BITE THE HAND

BITE THE HAND

A Play

Gavan Daws

EL LEÓN LITERARY ARTS

Bite the Hand is published by El León Literary Arts and
distributed by Creative Arts Book Company.
El León Literary Arts is a nonprofit public benefit corporation established to extend the array of voices essential to a democracy's arts
and education. The Overbrook Foundation's generous support is
gratefully acknowledged.

For information contact:
Creative Arts Book Company
833 Bancroft Way
Berkeley, California 94710
1-800-848-7789

ISBN 0-88739-536-8
Library of Congress Catalog Number 2002112479
Printed in the United States of America

NOTES

or

A FUNNY THING HAPPENED
ON THE WAY TO THE THEATER

Bite The Hand was suggested by a real event:

Two dolphins had been in captivity for years at a marine mammal research laboratory, being used as experimental animals. One night, secretly, some lab workers lifted them from their concrete isolation tanks and released them into the open ocean.

No one had ever done anything like that before. It created a furor. It made *Rolling Stone's* annual list of the most amazing happenings in the world. And it resulted in a one-of-a-kind criminal trial.

The story caught my eye. I knew nothing about dolphins, and less than nothing about dolphins in captivity. To begin with, I saw the event just as a highly unusual heist: How do you corral two seven-foot, four-hundred-fifty-pound marine mammals, active, fast-moving and powerful in the water, lift them from their tanks, now nine hundred pounds of dead weight, wrangle them out the door of the lab into the middle of a big city, transport them overland and deliver them, still alive, active and powerful, into the ocean an hour away—all totally unobserved?

The next question was: why? And the why promptly swamped the how. Ignorantly curious, I belly-flopped into what turned out to be a maelstrom of raging argument. Dolphins provoke fierce disagreements and bristling antagonisms among humans. Meeting and talking to people deeply involved with dolphins, I ran across a an extraordinary range of characters who were publicly and in the utmost seriousness playing out a complex array of private projections—from dolphin worshipers, convinced that dolphins hold the key to the universe and are telepathically transmitting their cosmic plans to certain privileged humans, to dolphin exploiters, including resort and theme park developers, and not excluding scientists staking out personal territory, armed with dueling heavy-caliber theories and propelled by rampant ambitions. Altogether a wild commotion of humans, riding off in all directions at once, on the backs of dolphins. As someone once remarked, reflectively, in a different context: What a piece of work is a man. (To which I would add, in the dolphin world, what a piece of work is a woman.)

The original release was the takeoff point for *Bite The Hand*. But only the takeoff point. Those two dolphins were lifted out of captivity deliberately to provoke a legal test case based on morality. Since then there have been other, differently motivated releases of captive dolphins, for purposes of scientific study. And yet other episodes, unintended: dolphins penned in ocean installations figuring out their own way to escape, some to be pursued and caught and returned to captivity, others just disappearing into the open sea.

All this I took under advisement.

I never saw the original two dolphins, but I did see many others in captivity. I concluded that just as the humans at tankside had distinguishable identifying personalities, so the dolphins captive in their control had distinguishable identifiable dolphinalities: they were insistently and inextinguishably individual. So here were disciplined big-brained terrestrial mammals laboring to bend often unmanageable big-brained marine mammals to their will. If you wanted to look at it this way (and I found I couldn't help it), inseparable from the seriously staged scientific work of the labs there was a kind of long-running deadpan interspecies comedy.

I also saw many other things that were much less amusing.

The dolphin behaviors in the play are reality-based, and so is the experimental research. Beyond that, the play is a work of the imagination, in which the characters, humans and dolphins alike, bear no intended resemblance to those at the real-life lab or anywhere else in the human-dolphin world.

Along with that disclaimer comes a consumer advisory: *Bite The Hand* is emphatically not kid stuff, a stage 'Flipper' or 'Free Willy.' It is for adults. The back and forth of public posturings and private passions. The pull and tug of argument. Serious ideas being subverted (with punchlines and pratfalls). All clustered around a magnetic ruling physical image, powerful and sensual.

*   *   *

Because the physical action of the play is so unusual, and because the research lab is a world unto itself, some guideposts will be helpful, here and in the text. (Directors and actors are of course free to follow these markers only as far as they choose and then strike out for themselves.)

The two captive dolphins are played by humans, one female, one male—dancers, capable of sinuous-sensuous-kinetic-ballistic movement, solo and together.

For other cast members, physical intelligence is also a priority: some of them turn into dolphins and back again into humans.

All costumes—dolphin and human, male and female—are identical, along the lines of dark-colored wet suits; and everyone is barefoot.

The set is minimal and in no way 'realistic' (beginning with—of course—no water in the two isolation tanks).

The lab apparatus that is talked about—computers, pumps, etc—is almost all imaginary.

The experiments on the dolphins are acoustic, so we do need some real sound equipment at tankside: two functioning consoles capable of generating electronic tones. And we need stereo speakers (in a real-life lab these would be hydrophones, underwater) to make the electronic tones clearly audible throughout the theater, so that the audience can mentally take part in the experiments. (An observed scientific fact: participating humans will find that they do not score as high as the dolphins.)

Also coming through the speakers will be dolphin sounds: whistling noises, and pulses of rapid-fire clicks. In one scene, open-ocean underwater sound is played to the dolphins.

When the dolphins 'dance,' as they do in key scenes, it is to electronic music: enhanced and manipulated dolphin sounds mixed with wild ocean sound.

In each tank we also need a *bite bar*. The bite bar is where the dolphins have been trained to station themselves for their experimental work sessions. The bite bars hang down low over the water on ropes, like trapezes. These trapezes make possible the dolphins' sweeping and spinning movements—the play's central element, visual, physical, emotional. The magic is in the movement.

TIME AND PLACE

Not quite then, not quite now

*A marine mammal research laboratory on the coast,
not exactly anywhere*

THE CHARACTERS

For scientific purposes, the captive dolphins have no
individual names. The female is referred to as ONE, the
male as TWO. In isolation they have developed behaviors like lifers in prison. ONE is doing straight time,
never bucking the system; but she has learned how to
work the system. TWO is the opposite kind of lifer. He
has chosen to resist, even if it means doing hard time.
And he is always scheming to subvert the system.

RUMMEL. A dolphin trainer with a lot of miles on the
clock. He runs the experimental sessions with Two.
Rummel is intelligent but quirky. It is hard to decide
what he is serious about. He seems feckless. Often his
lines sound like throwaways. Or maybe he is deflecting,
saying one thing but meaning another.

TRUBY. A brand-new PhD, fresh to the lab and fresh to
working with dolphins. He runs sessions with One.
Truby burns with a blue flame for science, and we might
think of him at first as wet behind the ears about life,

nothing but nerdly; but he has ambitions.

GRISSOM. He manages the lab. There is about him the whiff of an ex-career-military NCO. Over the course of the play, we come to realize that Grissom never intends to get in the water with a dolphin.

CELESTE. She wants to use dolphins for therapy swims with disabled and autistic children. She sees herself as on a gratifying, heartwarming mission. Her sense is that, being at the center of the universe, she naturally deserves to attract admiration. (Celeste can double in smaller parts; see below.)

DR. BAMBERGER. The lab's head scientist. A big name in behavioral psychology research. The experiments are his creations. The dolphins have made his reputation. We need to know about Bamberger, but we don't have to cast him, because we never see him in the flesh; he is always away on high-level scientific business.

Other parts can be doubled: watchers at the lab, friends of Rummel, The Law, The Media.

ACT ONE

1. OPENING SCENE

The lab is not yet set up. The stage is bare. Bite bar trapezes are tied back out of the way, not recognizable for what they are.

As the audience is gathering, the full cast is out amongst them in the aisles, playing the Training Game, an exercise that demonstrates and teaches the method used to train dolphins in captivity.

Cast members are paired: one the trainer, the other the 'dolphin.' The trainer asks an audience member to suggest a movement for the dolphin to learn, something simple like turning in a circle or jumping up and down or patting the head with the left hand. More elaborately, it could be unknotting the audience member's tie. The dolphin hasn't heard the assignment. To start with, it doesn't know what it is supposed to do. It just moves about. Every time it makes a move that is even slightly in the direction of the desired action, the trainer rewards it with a fish—positive reinforcement. No other movements are reinforced. In this way, the train-

er 'shapes' the dolphin's behavior, and by 'successive approximations' the result is reached. A trainer using food reward on a real dolphin in captivity can shape a behavior in fewer than twenty approximations.

After each success or failure, trainer and dolphin reverse roles.

The Training Game will teach the audience the training signals and dolphin actions that will be seen and repeated throughout the play: (i) the hand gestures used in the experiments, (ii) the trainers tossing a fish reward to the dolphins, and (iii) dolphins snapping up the fish.

Now, with the audience seated, the trainer-dolphin pairs move to the stage, to start setting up the lab.

Speech fragments here are chosen and orchestrated at director's discretion. Some lines will turn up again later in the play, some won't. If utterances overlap, that is all right. The only requirement is that lines marked * stand out sufficiently.

*—The animal has to understand—it isn't in the ocean any more.

—It's in a tank.

—We sailed with them.

—They stayed with us for hours.

—Hundreds and hundreds.

—I couldn't count them.

—It's by itself. It can't go anywhere.

—When the animal is hungry, it will work.

—Train by the clock.

—Sessions same time every day.

—The animal will be looking for you at those times.

—The animal will be hungry at those times.

—Motivated.

—That's it. Closer.

*—Give it a fish.

—He rolled over on his side and he looked up at me out of one eye, like he was saying, How's that?

—That's the reward.

—The reward is what the animal understands.

—An animal just captured from the wild may be unresponsive.

—Unwilling.

—Or plain defiant.

—Whoa. Catch the behavior.

—Blow the whistle and give it a fish.

—If the animal doesn't want to take the bite bar, tap it on the jaw and give it a fish.

—And then they swam away. I guess they were just checking us out.

—Don't rush it.

—Give it a fish.

—Hold your hand in the water.

—Throw the fish closer and closer, so the animal has to come closer and closer—

—To get the fish.

—*[overlapping]* Give it a fish.

—Reward the behavior you want, and no other behavior.

—Successive approximations.

—Food reinforcement, as little as possible.

—Ration it down.

—She was blowing bubbles.

—This great bubble.

—Like a balloon filled with light.

—She brought it up from the bottom of the tank.

—Up to the top, and she kept spinning it with her beak.

—She didn't even burst it . . .

—If the animal won't cooperate with you, don't cooperate with the animal.

—You've got to catch the behavior right at the peak.

—Take a time out.

—Turn your back.

—Cover the fish bucket.

—No work, no fish.

—Bring him down to eighty percent.

—Ease her onto it, so it takes her weight.

—So she doesn't strand.

—Give it a fish.

—I could hear the sounds coming through the water.

—Clicks.

—Long bursts.

—I could feel it pulsing.

—Whistles.

—They're intelligent.

—And quick.

—Quicker than you.

—They were playing, surfing—

—Caught the wave—

—Magic—

—In—out—in—out—

—Like a sailmaker's needle . . .

—Talk about sharp—

—They know where they're at.

—They know where you're coming from.

—My face right up next to hers.

—Just glued to her side.

—We were swimming round and round and she was doing body rhythms to the music.

—It has to let you touch it before it gets a fish.

—Catch the behavior. Put it on cue.

—And it just kept swimming around, holding the sick one up—brought it to the surface to breathe.

*—The animal has to *want* to come to the bite bar.

—Give it a fish.

—Let him have the ball.

—Drain the tank.

—Isolate the variables.

—Let her have the ball.

—He held onto my hand.

—Kept holding it under his pec.

—Wouldn't let me go.

—For hours.

—Don't indulge an animal that's not working.

—Get the ball.

—Eighty percent.

—Eighty percent of wild weight.

—She was making this little coughing sound.

—All night.

*—After thousands of repetitions the animal's limits have been tested and established.

—We know—

—[*overlapping*] It's all in the repetitions.

—[*overlapping*] That's where the truth lies.

—[*overlapping*] The truth lies.

—[*overlapping*] Repetitions.

—[*overlapping*] Lies.

—[*overlapping*] In the repetitions.

—And then . . . they swam away . . .

2. THE LABORATORY IS SET UP

Day.

FULL CAST now working fast to set up the lab—the two tanks, with a dividing platform between; hydrophones; a ladder to the offstage observation tower and computer room; a loudspeaker. No waste time or motion. GRISSOM climbs the ladder out of sight. Purposeful hustle-bustle continues. During all this, speech fragments from FULL CAST. Lines for GRISSOM and RUMMEL are specified.

Loudspeaker crackles.

GRISSOM: *[through the loudspeaker]* : You check the chlorine?

—Check.

GRISSOM: Copper sulfate?

—Yeah.

—Levels down, both tanks.

—High point scorer for the week is algae.

RUMMEL: Algae. Algae. Algae.

GRISSOM: Up the input. After tank-cleaning.

—What can you make them do?

GRISSOM: Rummel.

RUMMEL: Yeah, Grissom?

GRISSOM: Those people. Flakes. I don't want flakes hanging around the tanks.

RUMMEL: *[inaudible.]*

GRISSOM: No unauthorized personnel.

—Sundays, scrub out the tanks and swab down the concrete deck.

—Right.

—Visitors must be escorted.

—No exceptions.

Tanks are separated from each other now. Humans are climbing out, to become WATCHERS, sitting around the perimeter, observing, commenting, and from time to time joining the action.

ONE and TWO alone in their tanks. Our first sight of dolphin movement. Nothing like the full range of swings and sweeps and twirls, because the trapezes are not yet deployed—just movement on the floor, and slow, but enough to get us hooked by the idea of humans as dolphins.

—Do they know how long they've been in the tanks?

—It's all posted.

—Check the bulletin board.

—Sign in, sign out. Everybody.

—No exceptions.

—Look at their eyes.

—The longer they're around humans, the narrower their eyes get.

—And these are—

—Yeah—

—Narrow-eyed dolphins.

GRISSOM: Rummel. Locked and loaded?

RUMMEL: Sir.

GRISSOM: Hydrophones on.

RUMMEL: Sir.

The electronic consoles are the last things moved into place, one at each tank. RUMMEL walks to each of them in turn, makes switch-on motions—

Natural dolphin sounds cut in. Strange, and quite loud, to the point of being a bit startling. Distinctly separate in each tank. We hear rapid-pulse clicks only—no slow-pulse clicks, and no whistles.

—Hey, listen.

—Stick your head in the water—you can hear them.

—Click trains.

—Rapid pulse.

—Nothing but clicks?

—Rapid-pulse clicks.

—First few days in the tank, they whistle a lot, like in the ocean.

—Dolphins in a school.

—Whistling to each other.

—Sociability.

—This kid the other day, with his boogie board—stuck his head through the fence, and he said—

—Why do you keep them in those tanks?

—Highly social animals.

—But after a while—

—In the tank—

—In isolation—

—No more the whistling sound—

—No one there to answer—

—Just click trains.

—Rapid-pulse.

—Echo-locating.

—*[overlapping]* Echo-locating.

—Their sonar.

—They're sonaring the walls of the tank.

—*[overlapping]* Testing the walls.

—*[overlapping]* Keep doing it—

—[*overlapping*] All the time.

—Even at night . . .

3. DOLPHIN DANCE

Night.

The dolphin sounds turn into electronic music. Throughout the play, this change will signal the start of dolphin dances.

This first dance consists of solos for each dolphin isolated in its tank—simultaneous but separate and different. The pace is very slow.

Later dolphin dances will become more complex and striking.

This one finishes with music fading to silence, night falling, rest . . .

4. TIME IS TIGHT

Day.

RUMMEL moving onto the divide between tanks. GRISSOM offstage, up in the computer room, supervising over the loudspeaker. TRUBY to enter midscene. Remaining cast are WATCHERS. Speech fragments from them are interpolated.

During the day—in 'lab time'—when ONE is not called to do experiments, she circles her tank, at the edges, always counterclockwise, speed unvarying. This is what is called 'stereotyped behavior,' common among animals in captivity for long periods. TWO, by contrast, is not stereotyped in behavior like ONE.

RUMMEL leans over TWO's tank. He makes a little chirruping sound, which brings TWO instantly swimming his way.

RUMMEL: OK, Two. Cetacean aerobics. Company calisthenics before we punch the clock. Tail up. Come on. Up. Up. Good one. Have a fish.

He throws a fish. TWO snaps it up.

Loudspeaker crackles. Sound of mike being tapped.

GRISSOM: *[over loudspeaker]* Testing-one-two-three. Bamberger, Series Echo Fiver-Niner, Slash Zero Zero One . . . Rummel—

RUMMEL: Yeah?

GRISSOM: The console checks out?

RUMMEL: Operative.

GRISSOM: Review your signals.

RUMMEL: No change.

GRISSOM: So you tell me—

RUMMEL: Why would there be?—

GRISSOM: Dr. Bamberger says—self-review every day, and he wrote the book, so that's what we do, we self-review every day. Like I tell you every day. Changes creep in, the animal cues off the changes. You trainers get involved, you want the animal to do well, you *em-path-ize*, you make little helpful moves and you don't even know you're doing it, and all the time that cunning animal is cueing off your body language. Reading you, not doing the test. Things get bent out of shape. False productivity. Bad science. Fish for nothing. We don't never need that, and not at this point in time, that's for sure. So self-check. Show me.

RUMMEL: *[half-audibly]* Grissomobics 101.

RUMMEL faces the loudspeaker, and in response to commands from GRISSOM he makes the hand signals that constitute the command language for the experiment on Two.

GRISSOM: Approach the bite bar . . . Station . . . Make your response . . . Correct . . . Incorrect. A bit shabby. Rummelisms. Clean them up. Again.

> *RUMMEL continues to gesture as WATCHERS around the tanks imitate and repeat this gestural command language, varying the order, adding speech fragments.*

—Approach the bite bar.

—Station.

—Make your response.

—Yes.

—Correct.

—You've got to catch the behavior right at the peak.

—Or the animal doesn't know what it's being rewarded for.

—No.

—Incorrect.

—Yes.

—Incorrect.

—No.

—Correct.

—No.

—Yes.

—Give it a fish.

—Make your response.

> *TRUBY has been sitting among WATCHERS, not participating, speaking silently into his microcassette recorder. He clicks the recorder off, stands, and walks down to the edge of the tanks to watch RUMMEL.*

GRISSOM: *[his loudspeaker voice emerging through the overlapping speech fragments]* Approach the bite bar . . . Station . . . Make your response.

RUMMEL: Et cetera, et cetera, and so forth. *[To GRISSOM]* And that's all he wrote.

GRISSOM: Hmph . . . And you're rewarding by the—

RUMMEL: *[overlapping]*—By the book.

Now GRISSOM addresses TRUBY. RUMMEL continues making hand gestures briefly by himself, silently.

GRISSOM: *[over loudspeaker]* Truby, right?

TRUBY: Yes it is.

GRISSOM: The wonder boy. And right on time.

TRUBY: Yes I am.

GRISSOM: I'm coming down.

RUMMEL: *[shaking hands]* Rummel. How was the flight?

TRUBY: It took off, flew, landed, in the correct order. I got my reading done.

RUMMEL: [indicating lab, with a suggestion of training gestures in his motions] So—this is where it's at. Tanks. Computer room. Fish locker upwind, humans downwind. Wouldn't have been my personal choice of a design solution. I suppose they figured it was close enough for government work.

TRUBY: Dr. Bamberger says I'll be networked. And I am to have unrestricted access.

RUMMEL: Uh-huh. You'll be bunking over there. Downwind, but you get the marina view. You're with

One. I'm this side, with Two. Do you surf?

TRUBY: No.

RUMMEL: There's good surf.

GRISSOM has climbed down the ladder.

GRISSOM: [*shaking hands with a muscle grip that causes TRUBY to wince — Grissom likes to be thought of as the alpha animal*] Grissom.

TRUBY: Mr. Grissom. Dr. Bamberger gave me the protocol—the final version, superseding the beta. To study on the plane.

GRISSOM: And you're on top of it.

TRUBY: Yes I am.

RUMMEL: Bully for you, Truby.

TRUBY: Dr. Bamberger wishes me to impress upon you that time is tight, there is urgency, his exact words, so to load the program—

GRISSOM: I don't need to hear it from you, Truby. He's been e-mailin' me on the hour every hour—spamajama-rama.

TRUBY: The word around the commission, at the hearing, is that everyone is downsizing—*being* downsized, I mean. Grant money isn't flowing, research dollars are drying up. Funding for the next stage is problematical. But Dr. Bamberger is confident—if anyone can, he—

RUMMEL: Dr. Bamberger, he's the doctor.

TRUBY: Yes he is.

RUMMEL: He knows how to run that grant maze.

TRUBY: I should say, Rummel, Dr. Bamberger could have *designed* that maze. He has an aptitude—I would say an appetite—for complexity. I would rank him as *the* authority on the workings of the entire profession. As he put it to me at the hearing, privately, between sessions—How exactly did he phrase it? Yes—the cybernetics of grant renewal, feedback loops within feedback loops, the involved system of reciprocal favors that permeates peer review, is a construct as handsome and intricate as the whorls of the chambered nautilus. Captured it perfectly, in my opinion. I complimented him.

GRISSOM: Hey, that was down on paper I'd be movin' my lips on the big words.

TRUBY: Oh?

GRISSOM: It's above my pay grade. Me, I'm just Joe Sixpack here, Mr. Nine To Five. 'Downsizin',' though—*there's* a word comes through loud and clear. *That* I hear. What it tells me—put out, to the max, or asses will be grasses, and I'm talkin' my ass, which is near and dear to my heart. I got bills, got car payments, house payments, wife payments—

TRUBY: It is a challenge, yes—

GRISSOM: It's a galvanized son of a bitch.

TRUBY: Not the end of the world. By no means—

GRISSOM: A bad moon risin', how it looks to me—*[indicating RUMMEL with a flick of the head]*—He can give you the rest of the familiarization, the Rummel nickel tour. Tomorrow, Truby, 0800 hours, I brief you on firewalls and encryption, and we bear down, create some forward motion.

TRUBY: I'm looking forward—

But GRISSOM is through with him, and starts walking off toward the ladder.

RUMMEL: *[to TRUBY]* Grissomwise, what you see is what you get. Labwise—what you see—this is basically it. Tankwise, dolphinwise—One, Two—that's who really runs the place.

TRUBY: Ah.

He gravitates toward ONE's tank.

RUMMEL: Been here longer than Grissom, both of them. Old inhabitants. Longer than anyone but Bamberger— Bamberger was present at the creation. They know the ropes. They taught me all I know.

TRUBY: Ha.

He looks at ONE circling in her tank, counterclock-wise, speed unvarying. He takes out his recorder. RUMMEL, seeing this, raises an eyebrow slightly to himself.

TRUBY: *[speaking into recorder]* Identification. Tape One, Side One, Dr. Bamberger's project, Series E59. Marine Mammal Laboratory, Day One. Observations on arrival. Tanks—*[to RUMMEL]*—what—sixty feet across?

RUMMEL: Fifty.

TRUBY: And—

RUMMEL: Five foot deep.

TRUBY: Complying with regulations.

RUMMEL: Code minimum, as written, yeah. To the inch.

TRUBY: That goes without saying. Dr. Bamberger is nothing if not scrupulous. And he uses conventional bite bars?

RUMMEL: Yeah, he's stuck with them.

TRUBY: [*clicking off tape recorder*] Well, after all—

RUMMEL: —He wrote the book.

TRUBY: Yes he did. Which you have to respect. As I do. I mean, speaking as a professional myself, I find him admirable. And he *is* admired. Widely, in my observation. I think we could extrapolate and say universally.

RUMMEL: Like you said, he's the doctor.

TRUBY: And, my goodness, a personal invitation. Coming from him. When I applied—of course I wanted—wanted nothing more, who wouldn't—but think of the competition, especially now, with things as difficult as they are—Well, it was gratifying. Of course, he's a taskmaster—

RUMMEL: Famous for it in both hemispheres.

TRUBY: But that's precisely what distinguishes him, isn't it. The point is—what an opportunity. I mean, when I checked my e-mail, and up came his personal message, I dropped everything.

RUMMEL: Good job, Truby. You're not one to sit waiting, huh, for the second knock . . . Now, I've got this right?— you haven't worked with dolphins before?

TRUBY has gravitated to the console by ONE's tank, where he stands like an academic lecturer discoursing from a podium.

TRUBY: But Rummel, don't you see, that's Dr. Bamberger's very point. Classic operant conditioning techniques allow trans-species applicability. As he is fond of saying: The Laws Of Learning Are The Laws Of Learning. Techniques developed in work with chimps, or down the scale to rhesus monkeys, macaques—even pigeons, my dissertation study, which was what caught Dr. Bamberger's eye . . . And his new protocol. Elegant. When he and I publish—he will be the senior author, of course—

RUMMEL: Of course. The Alpha Animal.

TRUBY:—Porting everything over, so to speak, intact— better than intact, enhanced—to dolphin behavioral psychology.

RUMMEL: Skinner and water.

TRUBY: Ahaha. Skinner and water. Very good—*[He clicks on tape recorder and speaks into it.]*—Tankside. I was speaking briefly to Rummel, the incumbent—ah—trainer whom I have just met, explaining the trans-species applicability of Dr. Bamberger's operant conditioning techniques, up and down the evolutionary scale and across phyla and genera, in this instance from terrestrial species to marine mammals. And Rummel nimbly responded— ha—'Skinner And Water.' *[He clicks off the recorder.]* A provocative title for a conference paper, Rummel. I wonder how Dr. Bamberger would respond to it.

He looks at ONE.

TRUBY: *[continuing, taping again]* Observing One . . . It— she—is circling—

He walks alongside ONE, tracking her. She pays no attention to him, even when he goes ahead of her and turns to walk backward, putting himself in her line of sight.

TRUBY: *[continuing]*—Counterclockwise. Stereotyped behavior—something else we observe across species lines—I have seen it in my pigeons. I note—am I observing correctly, Rummel?—

RUMMEL: Yes you are.

TRUBY: Do I note some flaccidity of the dorsal fin?

RUMMEL: Yes you do. Some flaccidity.

TRUBY: She's been Dr. Bamberger's animal—how long?

RUMMEL: Ten years. Secondment from the Navy.

TRUBY: *[into recorder]* Ten years, secondment from Navy.

RUMMEL: The same for Two. That's when I came in. Long time, lots of miles on the clock. Just about out of the warranty period.

RUMMEL starts walking around TWO's tank, clockwise. He makes his chirrup sound, causing TRUBY to blink a little as TWO moves from the center to the edge of the tank and follows RUMMEL.

TRUBY: Dr. Bamberger's series of papers on One—classics, seminal. But do you know, it's just struck me—I'm embarrassed to confess I must have overlooked it—I don't believe I've ever had it fully explained to me.

RUMMEL: How's that?

TRUBY: Numbers for names—One, Two, and so on.

TRUBY and RUMMEL, having circled in opposite directions, meet on the platform between the tanks. ONE and TWO are on opposite sides of the divide, neither showing any sign of being aware of the presence of another dolphin.

TRUBY holds up his tape recorder to catch RUMMEL's response. RUMMEL speaks silently into recorder. WATCHERS interpolate speech fragments.

—Numbers.

—No names.

—Numbers.

—Personnel not to identify with a particular animal.

—Otherwise—

—Varying degrees of social reinforcement.

—Animals with each other during experimental period.

—More than one trainer with a single animal.

—Equals possible loss of control of reinforcement of the behavior.

Behind this, TRUBY has been silently dictating into his recorder, reviewing RUMMEL'S silent response.

TRUBY: *[normal voice now, into recorder]* Putting what Rummel has tried to explain into a more orderly sequence—in re numbers, not names. Dr. Bamberger insists upon that. Personnel are not to identify with a particular animal. Dr. Bamberger doesn't want varying degrees of social reinforcement, different trainers with the same animal on the same experiment. Or animals to have access to each other. Any or all of the above means possible loss of control of reinforcement of the behavior.

So—

RUMMEL: *[normal voice now]* By the numbers.

TRUBY: One—Two.

RUMMEL: One in one tank, Two in the other. I can see where he's headed—he's talked about it—to where the trainer isn't even visible, and the reinforcement is mechanical, from fish feeders.

TRUBY: Really. That *is* food for thought—*[into recorder]*— Flag for future reference—trainer not visible; reinforce mechanically, from fish feeders.

RUMMEL: Do you have a problem with that?

TRUBY: No I don't.

RUMMEL: Bully for you, Truby. And your grant is how long?

TRUBY: Six months. Extendable based on results. Not the most propitious fiscal environment. But that's true every-where. And what a privilege. To start my career, singled out by Dr. Bamberger. And the new protocol, with so much riding on it—I expect I don't have to tell you that. And to be trusted with his number one animal—

He is back at the console again, as at a lecture hall podi-um, looking at ONE circling in her tank—taking pos-session of his new domain.

5. DOLPHIN TRAINING

Day.

RUMMEL and TRUBY. The loudspeaker crackles. They turn toward it.

GRISSOM: *[through speaker]* Heads up. D-Day minus fifty and counting. Rummel, you're on. Truby, you're up next.

RUMMEL eases himself into TWO's tank, to work standing. When he speaks and gestures, it is as if he is instructing WATCHERS, and/or demonstrating to audience, though not realistically. TRUBY looks on, speaking silently into his recorder, repeating what RUMMEL is saying, conscientious and ambitious, taking good notes.

RUMMEL: It's easy enough to get the dolphin to move about the tank, or come close to the side of the tank. You just throw a fish where you want the dolphin to go. *[He holds up an imaginary fish.]* Cut fish. Dead fish. Vitamin-enriched. Frozen smelt. Where does the name come from, I hear you ask? From the past tense of the verb 'to smell.' Standard-issue lab food. It's all they get, and this is how they get it. From us.

He throws several fish in different directions, one at a time. TWO anticipates and effortlessly snaps them out of the air.

RUMMEL: *[continuing]* It's harder to get the dolphin to stay in one place in the center of the tank. But for acoustic experimental work the dolphin must station in one place—in the center of the tank, underwater. For this we use an apparatus called the bite bar . . .

He reaches up and unties the trapeze over TWO's tank. It comes shaking down.

TRUBY puts away his recorder, climbs down into ONE'S tank and looses the trapeze there in the same way.

RUMMEL: Now, coming to the bite bar and stationing— this is not natural behavior. You don't find it in the wild. The behavior has to be trained, it has to be *shaped*.

TRUBY and ONE begin moving in parallel with RUMMEL and TWO, but a beat behind—RUMMEL the teacher, TRUBY the student.

GRISSOM has come down the ladder from the computer room to observe. First he watches TRUBY, by

walking counterclockwise around ONE's tank. Then
he walks clockwise around TWO's tank, watching
RUMMEL.

RUMMEL: *[continuing]* The dolphin will approach the
bite bar out of curiosity. When it does—make the
approach signal and give it a fish.

He does so, with TRUBY copying him.

RUMMEL: *[continuing]* As the dolphin comes closer to
the bite bar, signal and give it a fish . . . now . . . closer . . .
now . . . closer . . . now . . . Successive . . . approximations.

TRUBY: Successive approximations.

RUMMEL: The dolphin must accept the bite bar, take the
bite bar in its mouth. Again, this is not a natural behavior—the behavior has to be *shaped.*

GRISSOM: The animal has to *take* the bite bar. It has to
accept the bite bar.

RUMMEL: The dolphin's jaws touch the bite bar. Make
the stationing signal, and give it a fish. Now, the dolphin
will not take the bite bar in its mouth *naturally.* So—tap it
lightly on the jaw with a fish . . .

TRUBY: It will open its jaws to accept the fish . . .

RUMMEL: Slip the bite bar in—

TRUBY: Slip the bite bar in—

RUMMEL:—Make the signal, and give it a fish . . . Soon the dolphin will come to the bite bar at the signal.

GRISSOM is now back at the ladder.

GRISSOM: When the animal will come to the bite bar and take the bite bar, it is ready.

TRUBY, soloing now, successfully brings ONE to the bite bar. She takes the bite bar and stations perfectly. TRUBY, very pleased with himself, gives her a fish reward. He is about to climb out of the tank when RUMMEL, already out, throws him a fish reward—it hits him in the chest, startling him.

6. GETTING EXPERIMENTS UP AND RUNNING

Day.

TRUBY AND RUMMEL still at consoles.

GRISSOM: *[over loudspeaker, tapping mike]* Let's go. Go, go, go.

*We will now hear for the first time the consoles pro-
ducing their pure electronic sound tones, the basis of
auditory memory experiments.*

*Our plan is that after this scene the audience will
understand i) the trainers' hand signals; ii) the particular dolphin movements that signify Yes and No
responses; and iii) the audience will have learned
enough to mentally take part in the acoustic experiments from now on.*

RUMMEL: Truby, you get to test the sound.

TRUBY: Right.

RUMMEL: Stick your head in the water.

TRUBY does, comes up blinking.

TRUBY: Nothing.

RUMMEL: Oh, shoot—I didn't turn on?

*He signals to TRUBY to do it again. TRUBY takes a
big breath, dunks his head, holds it under. RUMMEL
watches him, waits several seconds, turns on. We hear
our first sample of electronic tones. TRUBY super-*

conscientiously holds his breath for the longest time, pulls back up, takes a big gulp of air, nods affirmatively to RUMMEL, then stands and hops on one foot with head tilted to get water out of his ear.

RUMMEL: Truby, your test results are back from the lab. Positive for chlorine—your hair will go green. Positive for copper sulfate—your teeth will go black.

TRUBY: *[still hopping]* Huh?

RUMMEL: And anything the dolphin's got, you just got.

TRUBY freezes on one foot, then realizes this is a joke—or at least he hopes so. He unfreezes.

RUMMEL is starting the next lecture/demonstration, with gestures and electronic tones, again addressing WATCHERS and audience. He uses TWO as his subject.

RUMMEL: We're testing the memory of the dolphin. Bring him to the bite bar . . . I play a sequence of . . . five . . . different tones . . . I delay . . . The dolphin waits . . . Now I play . . . the question tone. Is the question tone one of the five I played before? Yes? . . . or No? Does the dolphin remember correctly? Yes . . . or No?

TRUBY: *[who has progressed fast and is training confidently*

with ONE] Now we must train the animal to answer the
question. Come to the bite bar . . . Play the five tones . . .
Then the question tone. Is the question tone the same as
one of the five? We cue the animal to emit a specific
behavior. This behavior will come to mean that the animal is saying Yes, the tone is the same . . . Correct.
Reward the animal with a fish.

RUMMEL: Again. Come to the bite bar. Five tones.
Question tone. Is the tone the same? Yes. The dolphin will
come to understand that when the tone is the same, and
it performs this particular behavior in response—indicating that it *knows* the tone is the same—it will get a
reward—a fish.

TRUBY: Is the tone the same? No. This one is different.
When the question tone is *not* the same as any previous
tone, and when in response the animal emits *that* particular behavior, indicating that it knows the tone is *not* the
same, the behavior will be reinforced by a fish reward.

GRISSOM comes down to observe and monitor.

*TRUBY and RUMMEL continue to repeat signals,
but speaking silently now, as WATCHERS, voicing
speech fragments, move down into the tanks.*

*In Trainer/Dolphin pairs they repeat the training
actions. In the process they reverse roles: human-dol-
phin-human. ONE and TWO take part in this, revers-
ing roles like the others, dolphin-human-dolphin.*

Electronic tones continue.

—Avoid natural sounds.

—Nothing in the experiment should be in the memory bank of the animal.

—Or have any special significance for the animal.

TRUBY: *[normal voice now]* You must convey to the animal what you want, unmistakably. And do not be tardy in reinforcing. It's textbook. You tell a dog to sit, and it does, but you are late saying 'Good dog,' and by then it's standing again, and it thinks you are reinforcing it for standing. By the same token, if you are early, premature, you will be reinforcing the animal just for trying—but trying what? Wagging its tail? You have to catch the behavior you want—right at the peak . . . *[he does]* . . . And never reinforce in advance. No promises, no praise, no food—especially no food—except as a reward for work, productive work, performed on cue. Everything must be earned.

—No such thing as a free fish.

TRUBY: *[continuing]* Otherwise you are rewarding—reinforcing—unproductive—self-indulgent—

—Dolphin welfare queens—

—Taxpayers' dollars.

—No such thing as a free fish.

RUMMEL: *[training one of the WATCHER dolphins]* The dolphin must learn that it has to go through the whole sequence correctly before it gets a fish.

TRUBY: *[training another WATCHER dolphin]* The animal must come to the bite bar. Station at the bite bar. Listen to the sequence of tones. Wait for the question tone. And give the correct response, Yes or No, before it earns a fish reward.

    GRISSOM goes back up the ladder.

—The animal must come to associate the stationing signal with the bite bar.

—And associate the bite bar with work.

—And associate work—

—And only work correctly performed—

—With the fish reward.

    During the following, WATCHERS withdraw from tanks, and ONE and TWO revert to being dolphins.

GRISSOM: *[over loudspeaker]* Rummel.

RUMMEL: *[not stopping his work with TWO, not turning his head]* Yeah.

GRISSOM: You're on sequence number—

RUMMEL: Seventy.

GRISSOM: And the program says eighty—

RUMMEL: By the end of the day. Ten more miles of hard road.

GRISSOM: So hump, Rummel. Productivity. Truby?

TRUBY: Yes.

GRISSOM: You're at—

TRUBY: *[pleased with himself for being ahead of RUMMEL]* Seventy-seven. Three to go. Accuracy eighty-four percent, and the curve is rising.

GRISSOM: Good job, Truby . . . OK, troops, comin' up— The number of tones in the sequence increases from five to six. Acknowledge.

As GRISSOM speaks, TRUBY and RUMMEL make adjustments to their consoles, TRUBY ahead of RUMMEL.

TRUBY: Check.

RUMMEL: Check.

GRISSOM: Delay time is extended by one increment. Acknowledge.

TRUBY: Check.

RUMMEL: Check.

GRISSOM: And the difference in the tones narrows one increment—you're at borderline fine discrimination now. Acknowledge.

TRUBY: Check.

RUMMEL: Check.

GRISSOM: And double check.

From WATCHERS, speech fragments.

—Raise the level of difficulty.

—Increase the number of tones.

—Narrow the difference in the tones.

—Lengthen the delay.

—The scientific point and purpose is—

—To push the animal to its limits.

—After thousands of repetitions—

—Its threshold will have been reached.

—The animal will have been tested to its limits.

—Worked to its limits.

—The truth is in the repetitions.

—The truth lies in the repetitions.

—What can be learned from this experiment, has been learned.

—Added to—

—The store of human knowledge.

—And a new experiment can be designed and begun.

—To the limit.

GRISSOM: [*still over speaker*] Troops—only thirty shopping days to Christmas. I want those results comin' through slick as goose grease, no hiccups. Two steps forward, no steps back. And Rummel—

RUMMEL: Yeah?

GRISSOM: Daily event reports *on* the desk in the computer room. Don't seem like that's a natural behavior with you. Has to be shaped.

Pause. Loudspeaker crackles.

GRISSOM: *[continuing]* OK. That's mine for the day. I'm through. Over—and out of here.

Loudspeaker crackles and goes silent.

RUMMEL and TRUBY each finish a last run and switch off the consoles.

7. TANK TALK

Day.

The moment ONE's work day is ended, she leaves the bite bar and resumes her stereotyped circling of the periphery of her tank, counterclockwise.

RUMMEL, walking ahead of TRUBY to the platform, makes his chirrup sound, and TWO follows him.

RUMMEL and TRUBY sit on the platform. TWO is

right below RUMMEL, nosing up at him.

TRUBY: *[clicking on recorder]* That whistle, whatever you call it.

RUMMEL: Arthur? . . . No, it doesn't have a name.

TRUBY: What's the story?

RUMMEL reaches out and clicks recorder off.

RUMMEL: Between you and me, that's between Two and me.

TRUBY: It's not in the protocol—

RUMMEL: There are more things in heaven and earth, Truby, than are dreamed of in Bamberger's protocol. Doesn't scan right for Shakespeare, but it's true.

TRUBY: *[shakes his head, puts down recorder]* So—I'm interested anyway.

RUMMEL: In the spirit of scientific inquiry.

TRUBY: Yes I am. Of course.

RUMMEL: So, OK—I'd be strolling by and Two would bounce up out of the water, tail-walking, making all sorts of sounds. Obviously to get me to respond. So I picked one of those sounds he made to be my name, and when that sound came—*[he chirrups]*—I would turn around and go to the edge of the tank. And pretty soon Two learned that he didn't have to make all those other sounds. If he just made that one sound, I would come. And *I* learned that if *I* made that sound—my imitation of his sound—*he* would come. So that's what we do. Happy hour. He seems to enjoy it. And I . . . seem to enjoy it too.

TRUBY: Has Dr. Bamberger seen it, seen you doing this?

RUMMEL: When would he? When is he here?

TRUBY: He has pressing obligations, Rummel. In the higher reaches of the profession. And he's the principal scientist. It's his prerogative to delegate—it's time-and-energy-efficient—

RUMMEL: You know that story about Kissinger?

TRUBY: Henry—?

RUMMEL:—The good Doctor K. *[He picks up TRUBY's recorder, clicks it on and speaks into it.]* Back when he was at Harvard, he was teaching this graduate seminar, about the exercise of power, what else, and he was forever intoning 'Washington Is Calling,' and he would go shuttling off, short notice, Very Important Personage, Kissinger Rising. And when he was going to be gone, which was more often than not, he would scrupulously tape a lecture for the class—remote control freak—and the recorder would be sitting on the table, speaking words of wisdom, for the students to be taking notes.

And one day, back he comes, unexpectedly—they gave a crisis but nobody came or something—and there's no one in the seminar room, just his recorder, talking, and all around the table are these other recorders . . .

He clicks the recorder off and gives it back to TRUBY.

TRUBY: Is that true?

RUMMEL: It's a parable.

TRUBY: Ha. Ahaha. Though I'm not sure I see it as strictly analogous. Dr. Bamberger has his own good reasons. He's the responsible authority—it's prudent for him to be on the spot to monitor the grant extension—you know how time-consuming that process is—

RUMMEL: Slow, yeah. And ugly. Like watching a rat go through a snake.

TWO has been feeling neglected. He does a tail splash to get attention. RUMMEL chirrups. TWO responds.

TRUBY: Does Grissom know, then?

RUMMEL: Grissom-wise, me-wise, everything's on a need-to-know basis. Grissom's strictly a nine-to-five man, five days. I'm twenty-four hours, seven days . . . So are you.

TRUBY: But it amounts to variable social reinforcement. Doesn't that make it, by definition—how to put this—less than scrupulous? I mean scientifically. I always remember—Dr. Bamberger accepting the award: 'It is commonly held in our profession that scientific rigor—scrupulosity in even the smallest of small things—is a life-and-death-matter. I don't hold with such an attitude. It's *far* more important than that.'

RUMMEL: Ha. Ahaha. 'God is in the details' doesn't cut it with Bamberger. He's got details in the details in the details . . . Christmas, right after the award, he sent all the permanents a custom T-shirt with 'Far More Important Than That' on it. One size fits all or none. I Goodwilled mine.

TRUBY: Why ever would you do that?

RUMMEL: Not my color.

TRUBY: But that's what empowers Dr. Bamberger's work, isn't it? That dedication. I've seen it. Personally. You would not be aware of this, how could you be, but he invited the finalists to dinner, at his home. Part of the elimination process. After coffee I asked if we might visit his study. I mean, Rummel, that's hallowed ground. He led us upstairs. He sat at his desk, with his notes for the new protocol spread out, and launched into an exegesis of the subtleties of variable reinforcement. Brilliant. Vintage Dr. Bamberger. And I made an observation that piqued his interest, a contribution, and he reached for his pen and noted it—he uses a gold-nib Sheaffer Lifelong—

and then he looked up, in thought, and then he leaned forward and wrote again . . . and continued writing . . .

RUMMEL: *[to himself]* The shark must keep moving forward or it dies.

TRUBY: Mmmh? After some little time passed, actually quite some time, I thought it best—I took it upon myself—the initiative—I caught—as inconspicuously as I could manage—the eye of the others, and signaled to them unobtrusively, and led them quietly downstairs and ushered them out.

RUMMEL: And now here you are.

TRUBY: Yes I am.

RUMMEL: Truby to Bamberger, pigeons to dolphins—who's on first?

TRUBY: *[nettled]* It's not a game, Rummel. Not to me. But yes, I'm frank to say I am interested to cover bases, to move ahead. I'm using the present study to look beyond the present study. *[He stands.]* If I can see farther—

RUMMEL:—It is because, as they say, you're standing on the shoulders of, as they say, dolphins. *[Still sitting, he raises his eyes to TRUBY.]* Truby, I have to look up to you.

> *TRUBY starts to follow ONE. She is still circling. As he paces to catch up with her, she speeds up somewhat, not looking back at him.*

RUMMEL stays tankside, looking down at TWO. He puts his hands behind his back, then brings out first one hand, then the other, for TWO to tag with his beak, a little game. As RUMMEL alternates hands random-ly, varying the pace from slow to fast, we perceive that TWO is always in the right place a moment before RUMMEL's hand appears.

TRUBY breaks off from pursuing ONE and goes and sits among WATCHERS, silently speaking into his recorder, his head moving back and forth, watching ONE circling and TWO playing with RUMMEL.

Electronic music starts.

TRUBY freezes, head turned to look at ONE. RUM-MEL throws a fish into the middle of TWO's tank. TWO rolls away to it, and stays motionless. On the platform RUMMEL rolls over and freezes in sleep.

8. DOLPHIN DANCE

Night.

Dolphins dance, separate solos, brief.

A curious fact: dolphins never sleep, they are never absolutely still. At night they go into a kind of reverie, perhaps a dreaming condition, porpoising to breathe.

This dance reflects the reverie state.

ONE, even in her reverie dance, continues to follow a counterclockwise direction, but with much more pleasurably sinuous and languid movements than her daytime stereotyped swimming.

9. THE DEPTHS

Day.

As the electronic music fades to silence, TRUBY unfreezes, puts away his recorder and walks to RUMMEL, who is waking and stretching but not getting up.

TRUBY: Tank cleaning. You're in charge.

RUMMEL: Hark—it is the sound of Truby in the morning. He speaks, I apprehend, I apperceive his words. But can it be true—I'm in charge?

TRUBY: It's posted. Grissom has put you in charge.

RUMMEL: Grissom has put—me—in charge? Modified rapture! I'm really in charge?

TRUBY: You heard me.

RUMMEL: OK then, Truby—you do it.

TRUBY jogs RUMMEL with his foot, ungently. RUMMEL gets up amiably, stretches, and with arms out takes a 360-degree look around the two tanks.

ONE is circling. TWO is on the far side of his tank, as far away as he can get, not moving.

RUMMEL: Six days we work you. And on the seventh we strand you. Such is life.

He walks to each tank in turn and unscrews imaginary valves, to start the tanks emptying.

WATCHERS come to tankside with imaginary brushes, buckets, mops, squeegees.

RUMMEL and TRUBY join in swabbing down the surrounds of the tanks. They are territorial, RUMMEL working by TWO's tank and keeping an eye on him, TRUBY the same for ONE.

RUMMEL: *[to TRUBY]* Two doesn't like this. Not one bit. Right up there with the dog knowing he's on the way to the vet. Every week for ten years. That's five hundred-plus strandings, and how many more coming. And not a thing he can do about it. He hates it.

TRUBY: One is a good soldier. She goes with it.

RUMMEL: One will do anything for the fish. One is fish-driven. One thinks science is an elaborate mechanism for converting frozen smelt into One.

The water level is going down, draining from the outside of the tanks toward the middle, where the drain holes are. The dolphins' movements are starting to become constricted. ONE is swimming in tighter circles, because the water at the edges is getting too shallow.

TRUBY: I'm at the black line.

RUMMEL: OK. Go.

TRUBY climbs down into ONE's tank, and stands in the center by the trapeze, throwing fish to ONE, shorter and shorter. ONE takes them, coming closer and closer.

RUMMEL climbs down into TWO's tank, stands by the trapeze, and chirrups to TWO, with no result.

TRUBY: [*voice raised, to cover the distance between tanks*] That whistle behavior—you and Two. Two and you. It's not without interest, you know.

RUMMEL chirrups again—no response from TWO.

TRUBY: [*continuing*]   It's not in the protocol, and of course I must reserve judgment on that . . . aspect of things. But in and of itself it's not without interest— allowing the animal to set the terms of interaction.

RUMMEL is walking through shallow water to TWO at the far edge of the tank.

RUMMEL: [*to TWO*] Hear that, Two? Setting the terms of interaction. That fits right in with your plans, huh?

TWO can't move freely now. RUMMEL tries to encourage him toward the center of the tank. TWO is uncooperative, lying there, twitching minimally, essentially dead weight.

RUMMEL gives up. He motions to WATCHERS, and they climb into the tank, muttering under their breath.

One each side of TWO, one at his tail, RUMMEL at his beak, they crowd him toward the center of the tank, grunting with the effort. TWO flails around, hating this.

RUMMEL: [*voice raised, to TRUBY*] If I've told Grissom

once, I've told him a hundred times. The holding tank should be deeper. We shouldn't be stranding them. They're lying with their body weight on their lungs. They have to lift their whole weight to take a breath. Four hundred fifty pounds. It'd be like having an offensive lineman and a half standing on your lungs.

TRUBY: And what does Grissom say?

RUMMEL: He says what Bamberger says. It meets minimum standards. It's in the Bamberger manual. And it's in the Bamberger manual because it's in the Navy manual. So we strand them.

By now each dolphin is under the trapeze at tank center, an area doubling as the holding tank.

RUMMEL: *[continuing, to TRUBY]* How're you doing?

TRUBY: All the way down.

ONE has draped herself over the trapeze, stranded, acquiescent. TRUBY gives her a fish, then another.

TRUBY: *[continuing]* She's there.

RUMMEL and WATCHERS finally coax TWO to hang draped over the trapeze.

RUMMEL gives TWO some fish, one after the other. TWO accepts them grudgingly.

WATCHERS withdraw from tank.

RUMMEL: *[to TWO]* If I was running this place, I'd have . . . live fish . . . little caves . . . time off for good behavior . . . conjugal visits . . . vacations . . . The Bahamas, what do you say? . . . lounging at poolside . . . all the shrimp cocktail you can eat . . . great social life . . . You know, it's not true what they say about false killer whales, there was a big tour group of them at the casino, very warm people . . .

TWO hangs stranded—helpless, completely motionless, like a side of meat on a hook.

RUMMEL: *[continuing, to TRUBY]* Man, he's so far out of it, you think he's never coming back. Not a twitch. You could draw a line around him. Like a crime scene . . . *[more to himself now]* . . . 'Well,' said the mouse, as they strapped him in the rocket, 'it beats cancer research'— *[checking his watch, louder voice, to TRUBY]*—Let's get it on.

RUMMEL and TRUBY start scrubbing the tank walls with imaginary brushes, working hard and quick so as not to leave the dolphins stranded any longer than they have to. It is the fastest we have seen RUMMEL move. He pauses only to go check on TWO, scooping up handfuls of water to wet down his back.

RUMMEL: *[to himself as he scrubs, but getting louder and louder]* Algae. Algae. Algae. Algae. Algae. Between the toes, under the fingernails, in the eyebrows, in the armpits, in the ears, in the nostrils, in the navel, in the crotch, in the innermost crevices, the deepest convolutions of the brain. Algae. Algae. Algae. Algae-algae-algae. The man said—coming along behind the elephant with his scooper—'Another day like this and I'm gonna be thinking seriously of getting out of show biz.' Algae. Algae-algae-algae. The heartbreak of algae. Algaealgaealgaealgae. Algae.

Finished, he straightens up, and chirrups to TWO—no response. He walks to center tank, wets down TWO's back.

As he walks to the edge of the tank and hoists himself out, speech fragments from WATCHERS.

—Four hours to drain.

—An hour stranded.

—Four hours to refill.

RUMMEL twirls the drain valve in his tank, starting the refill.

RUMMEL: *[voice raised to TRUBY]* Refilling.

TRUBY: OK.

TRUBY twirls the drain valve of his tank and joins RUMMEL on the platform.

TRUBY: That—is—dirty—work. *[He scrapes algae off his arms and examines his hands with distaste.]* Dirty. Work.

RUMMEL: They didn't fill you in on this at the interview? Full disclosure?

TRUBY: No.

RUMMEL: The large print giveth, and the small print taketh away. Tom Waits.

TRUBY: Ha.

RUMMEL: *[picking algae off the back of his head]* Yeah, it's for the lower forms of life all right. Only *medulla oblongatas* need apply.

He chirrups to TWO. No response.

TRUBY: As I was saying—in connection with that whistle—allowing the animal to set the terms of the interaction. It's not in the protocol. But in a different context—
still controlled, of course—one might observe the animal
emitting some interesting behaviors . . .

> *Pause, with TRUBY waiting for RUMMEL to
> respond, which he doesn't.*

RUMMEL: Black line and rising

> *RUMMEL chirrups to TWO, who is still hanging over
> the trapeze, but with enough water beneath him now to
> stir into motion.*
>
> *The same is starting to happen with ONE.*

TRUBY: With an event recorder, optimally even a video
camera—

RUMMEL: Truby, please, just the harvest of your
thoughts—we can dispense with the ploughing and the
harrowing.

TRUBY: I suppose what I'm saying is . . . I suspect it could
be worked up into something publishable.

RUMMEL: And as between the two of us, you would see

yourself as the senior author.

TRUBY: Well—

RUMMEL: That's an observable behavior you keep emitting.

TRUBY: [*nettled*] There you go again, Rummel, making perfectly proper professional ambition sound like a dirty word—[*rubbing at algae on his thighs*]—At least I know what I want to do, what I want to accomplish, where I want to go.

RUMMEL: How do you spell Truby? N-O-B-E-L?

TRUBY: Come on, Rummel. What about your own observable behaviors? Who in the profession has ever heard your name? Rummel? Rummel? [*He moves his head back and forth like a dolphin, with his hand cupped to his ear, listening.*] No echo comes back to me. The name of Rummel is not heard in the land.

RUMMEL: I'm famous among my friends. Famous in two zipcodes. Less famous in one than the other, but I'm cool with that—

TRUBY: Have you ever published a scholarly paper?

RUMMEL: You got me there, Truby.

TRUBY: Correct. Have you ever designed an experiment?

RUMMEL: Wow, you really know how to hurt a guy.

TRUBY: Look how long you've been here—ten years, you say—and how far you've risen—you've got the key to the fish locker, and every week you're up to your armpits in algae.

RUMMEL: Hey, Truby, don't be pounding on a dead smelt. So I'm a slow learner. It took me all that time to work up to this. When I was a kid I used to throw rocks at chickens. I liked that fine, but I never had the arm to get to the top. Then for a while there I leaned toward a career in a bait shop, but you gotta have connections. Then I thought to try out for a dolphin. Failed the physical. And the intelligence test—undersize brain. On the evolutionary scale they classified me *Pithecanthropus Laboratorius*. Gave me a room, out of kindness, I suppose, a roof over my head. It's not much, but it's home.

TRUBY: A chicken coop.

RUMMEL: Come on. It rates at least a—a—piano crate.

TRUBY: And knee-deep in junk.

RUMMEL: *Pithecanthropus Pre-Domesticus.* Where man is, there shall junk also be. But hey, it's a meditation, it's a Stephen Wright koan: 'If I had everything, where would I put it?' Look, I've got surf right outside. Good, good surf. Sun comes in the window in the morning, warms my toes, wakes me up, and first thing I see is dolphins... And there's always girls wanting to check out the dolphins... No end of girls... *Pithecanthropus Fortunatus Erectus.*

TRUBY: Rummel—

RUMMEL: Fanatical dolphin groupies. Have to drive them off with squirt guns—

TRUBY: Rummel?—

RUMMEL: This one girl, she used to come bouncing in, do handsprings all the way around the tanks, no panties, bounce out again—

TRUBY: Rummel!—*[giving him the approach bite bar signal]*—Can I have what passes for your attention? The dolphin is a fascinating object of scientific study. A highly-evolved marine mammal. That big brain—forty million years of evolution produced that big brain. What is in that big brain? It is begging us to find out—to be useful to us. Dr. Bamberger is a towering figure—he's a—a—clear light, a beacon. And you—you know, Rummel, despite all, you don't strike me as unintelligent—yet if I observe correctly, you appear to be utterly incapable of finding stimulation in anything in your situation here beyond—sex and surfing.

RUMMEL: Sex and surfing. Hey, that's got a nice ring to it—alliterative. It works for dolphins in the wild. And the way I score it on the human scale, it's better than the national average.

TRUBY: But—you're *aimless*, Rummel. You're *drifting*. Where will you be in five years? Still grubbing around at the bottom of the tank? Where do you want to be?

RUMMEL: I dig where you're coming from, Truby. I hear you speaking for yourself—'It's hard to soar like an eagle when you're up to your ass in algae.' I can respect that. Me, I'm just makin' up my life as I go along. Sittin' on the dock of the bay . . .

He drops down into the tank.

He wades to TWO, still draped over the trapeze, takes hold of him, walks backwards and then releases him to swing back and forth, the beginnings of free movement again in water deep enough to swim.

TRUBY does the same for ONE, releasing her from the trapeze. She immediately goes back to circling.

Loudspeaker crackles.

TRUBY and RUMMEL come out of the tanks and go their separate ways to the consoles, TRUBY shaking his head over RUMMEL.

10. A FAILURE TO COMPUTE

Day.

Without ceremony, RUMMEL and TRUBY are back into the experiments. There is static in the air between them.

GRISSOM: *[over loudspeaker]* Go to seven tones. Acknowledge.

TRUBY: Check.

RUMMEL: Check.

After some repetitions, it will be clear to the audience that i) the dolphins now have to listen to seven tones instead of the original five, ii) that the tones are much closer in pitch, therefore much harder to tell apart, and iii) that the delay before the dolphins are asked to indicate Yes or No is a lot longer—altogether making the test much harder.

If we have an audience of average humans mentally taking the test, many will now be failing, scoring below fifty percent correct.

TWO is now slower than ONE, finicky about coming to the bite bar; and when he makes an incorrect choice he thumps the bar hard.

RUMMEL more than once makes the signal for Time Out to get TWO to calm down before the next run.

Meanwhile TRUBY is steaming ahead with ONE.

Loudspeaker crackles.

GRISSOM: [*over loudspeaker*] Hold it, hold it. Truby—where are you at?

TRUBY: Ahead of schedule. Comfortably.

GRISSOM: Hold it. You're gonna have to go back.

> *TRUBY gives the Time Out signal to ONE.*

TRUBY: What do you mean, go back?

GRISSOM: It's the motherin' computer. Motherin' hard drive. Bad motherin' sectors. Corrupted motherin' files. We've lost all today's data, and looks like back as far as—

TRUBY: Aargh.

> *TRUBY makes another Time Out signal to ONE, and walks in a contained little stereotyped counterclockwise circle.*

GRISSOM: Bamberger's steamed, you know how he gets, e-mail overload, fax overload, voice mail overload, system overload. 'The clock is tick-ing, the clock is tick-ing.' Hell, he's got no call to be ridin' me. I don't need any big deal hot dog scientist to tell me the little hand's here and the big hand's there and the clock is ticky-tockin'—

TRUBY: How long is it going to be down?

GRISSOM: Gonna to have to fly a tech in. So—two days, minimum.

TRUBY: Not good. Not good at all. *[He stops circling.]* Go back—how far did you say?

GRISSOM: The last data uncorrupted is at 225. There on, it all turns to dolphin shit.

TRUBY: Oh, *grunt*. Repeat from 226. And record results manually. *Grunt.* Manual recording all by itself is going to eat up time. *Double grunt.*

GRISSOM: So do the grunt work, Truby. Don't be sittin' on your thumb, twistin'.

> *TRUBY turns away from the loudspeaker and makes a face, but goes back to experiments with no wasted time or motion, silently.*

GRISSOM: *[continuing]* Rummel—

> *RUMMEL is watching something strange, that we have never seen before. TWO is not eating a reward fish, but is bringing it back and throwing it out of the tank at RUMMEL's feet.*

RUMMEL makes a Time Out signal to TWO, and turns to loudspeaker.

GRISSOM: *[continuing]* Bamberger wants to hear from you. What's this falloff with Two? He wants to know how come. All of a sudden Two's dropped back down to fifty percent, and that's not worth diddly squat. No better than random, no better than chance. Bamberger wants to know what the chlorinated hell you think you're doin'.

RUMMEL: *[making the Time Out signal]* Let me get this straight now. When the data are good—the curve is up—I have nothing to do with that, it's Bamberger's brilliant protocol, a genius plan for execution by idiots, Rummel-proof. And then all of a sudden the curve is down, and it's me?

GRISSOM: Well, somethin's come seriously unwrapped with Two. What is it?

RUMMEL: It's not in my job description to interpret or suggest. I just execute and report. You and Bamberger negative-reinforce me often enough on that one.

GRISSOM: So—report, Rummel.

RUMMEL: Have you keyboarded that last batch of event records? The ones I left *on* the desk in the computer room?

GRISSOM: Affirmative.

RUMMEL: And you sent the output to Bamberger?

GRISSOM: *[a pause]* Negative. Not yet.

RUMMEL: Well, come on down here. Bring those chlorinated event reports, and I'll give you something super-chlorinated for Bamberger.

TRUBY: *[to RUMMEL]* What are you talking about?

RUMMEL does not answer. Instead, with TRUBY watching, he runs a sequence with TWO. Approach signal. Stationing signal. Seven tones. Wait. Question tone. TWO is very slow to respond. Finally TWO lethargically produces the behavior for Yes. It is incorrect, and he gets no fish reward.

RUMMEL: Incorrect. That's one.

RUMMEL goes through another sequence, with TWO responding incorrectly again, slower still. Again no fish reward.

RUMMEL: Incorrect. That's two.

Another sequence. For the third time, TWO responds incorrectly, and slower still. Yet again no fish reward.

*GRISSOM arrives tankside in time to see this last one.
He is holding computer printouts.*

RUMMEL: And that's three. *[to Grissom]* Three in a row
incorrect.

GRISSOM: So what?

RUMMEL: So this.

*RUMMEL goes through three more sequences. TWO
responds slower and slower, but correctly to all three,
and gets rewarded.*

RUMMEL: Three in a row correct. After three in a row
incorrect. *[GRISSOM and TRUBY look at each other.]* Now
check the event reports.

*GRISSOM lays out fanfold computer paper on the
ground. He and TRUBY squat to inspect it. TRUBY is
clearly quicker of eye.*

TRUBY: *[the onset of incredulity]* Am I observing what I
think I'm observing?

RUMMEL: Depends on what you think you're observing.
Heisenberg. Or someone a whole lot like Heisenberg.

TRUBY: *[turning fanfold sheets back and forth]* He peaks in productivity and accuracy—here. Excellent levels. Better than One—which I would not have anticipated. But then he starts to fall off. And it's straight-line. Steep. Downhill all the way. To fifty percent—no better than chance. It makes no sense—

TRUBY goes on riffling sheets. GRISSOM looks at the sheets TRUBY has already seen.

GRISSOM: Holy—it's fallin' off the cliff—

TRUBY:—What is this? What *is* this? He bottoms out—here—at fifty percent. And from then on—he's been doing three correct, three incorrect, three correct, three incorrect?

RUMMEL: Correct. You are observing correctly.

TRUBY: You're telling me it's an—*intention*?

RUMMEL: Correct. Yes I am.

TRUBY: He *means* it?

RUMMEL: Correct. Yes he does.

TRUBY: He's *counting*?

RUMMEL: Correct. Yes he is.

TRUBY: Grissom—there's no way it can be an artifact of the computer?

GRISSOM: No way known to man or beast or even Rummel.

RUMMEL: Pay attention. He's sending Bamberger a message. Listen—

> *RUMMEL turns on the hydrophone in TWO's tank. Audience will hear i) underwater experimental sounds, ii) two different sounds that will be made by TWO.*
>
> *RUMMEL starts running three more sequences.*
>
> *By now, the audience knows the test well enough to be able to distinguish 'same' tones from 'different.' In these three tests, the first correct response is a 'same,' the next is a 'different' and the third is a 'same.' Above water, TWO responds wrongly for all three. But here's the thing. Underwater—that is to say, not perceptible by the trainer in the normal course of events—TWO gives out a burst of sound for each, one kind of burst signaling 'same,' another kind of burst signaling 'different.' That is, he gets all three right.*

RUMMEL: Hear that? Underwater he's scoring a hundred percent.

GRISSOM: *[realization dawning]* He's—screwin' with us!

TRUBY: *[unwilling to believe]* Again, Rummel.

> *RUMMEL starts another series of three.*
>
> *TRUBY puts his head under water to listen, coming up between each of the three tests. We hear the test sounds—and TWO's bursts of sound—indicating he is getting everything correct underwater and giving wrong indications above water. After the third, TRUBY surfaces with his mouth open, speechless, shaking his head.*

RUMMEL: That's the bad news. Now for the bad news. This just started—

> *RUMMEL does one more test. TWO gets it correct, snaps his fish reward out of the air, but does not eat it—he carries it betweeen his teeth to the edge of the tank, and with a flick of his head throws it at the feet of the watching humans.*

GRISSOM: Three-this, three-that—I plainly don't know what's in that can of worms. But this other business—an animal throwin' fish in my face—that constitutes weirdness, weirdness, not to mention unnatural discourtesy. What it says to me, Rummel, you've been overfeedin' him.

RUMMEL: No.

GRISSOM: Can I trust you on that?

RUMMEL: Have you weighed him? When did you weigh him last?

GRISSOM: Bamberger, you know what he says—it's not time-cost-effective.

RUMMEL: Bamberger doesn't believe in sensory invariety either. He wouldn't recognize sensory invariety if it tail-walked up to him and bit him in the left buttock. But that's what we're seeing. You know what Two's saying? 'I've been on this job too long. This same old same old same old is driving me crazy. I'm not going to work, not even if I don't get to eat. Screw you, and the frozen fish you rode in on.' That's what he's saying—'Take this job and shove it.'

GRISSOM: And you know what I say? Hear this, Rummel. No way. No way. This whole catastrophe—we got to get back on track, and I mean *yesterday*—computer, damn animal, the whole nine yards. No results, no grant renewal. No grant renewal, no dollars. No dollars, no jobs. No job, no paycheck, and it's my job I'm talking here, my paycheck, near and dear to my heart. That's how it computes to me. And how it computes for that damn animal is—no work, no fish. Take him down to eighty percent.

TRUBY: *[with tape recorder]* Grissom, just so I'm sure I'm getting this right. Eighty percent—you mean reduce the animal's food twenty percent?

GRISSOM: Straight out of the manual. Unless and until Bamberger tells me different. And I know he's not gonna tell me different. A hungry animal is an animal that will work. On that you can rely. 'The clock is tick-ing'—*[looking at watch]*—It's what time there? I might just catch him. If I don't, I'll message him to get back to me in the mornin'—urgent. *[He takes off for the ladder and climbs it at speed.]* I don't need *any* of this.

TRUBY: *[with recorder, to RUMMEL]* Eighty percent?—

RUMMEL: You didn't read Appendix 4? In the back of the manual? The small-print-taketh-away part? They catch the dolphin, and first thing in the tank they ration him down in food to eighty percent of his wild weight. Get him seriously interested in the idea of fish reward, concentrate his mind. No workee, no fishee.

TRUBY: But that's standard practice—doesn't matter what kind of animal—

RUMMEL: Right. You knew that, didn't you, Truby. And now they're going to take him down to eighty percent of that again—eighty percent of eighty percent of wild weight.

Loudspeaker crackles.

GRISSOM: *[over loudspeaker]* Listen up. I caught him.

Here's the word. And the word is bad. We are movin' deeper and deeper into dolphin doodoo. The commission has voted on that damn recommendation. They've revised the standards for the next grant period. Upwards. Bottom line, we've got to be producin' more data, more quicker, or we're not gonna be qualifyin'. Bamberger says extra sessions. Both tanks.

RUMMEL: Extra sessions? Two's over the edge now.

GRISSOM: Extra sessions.

RUMMEL: And the eighty percent of eighty percent?

GRISSOM: That stands.

RUMMEL: Wah.

GRISSOM: Write your congressman. But hereafter and nowafter, startin' tomorrow, extra sessions and eighty percent of eighty percent. Or there ain't gonna be no thereafter . . . I'm outa here.

Loudspeaker crackles and goes silent.

RUMMEL stands and considers, then heads for the fish locker and comes back with a bucket of fish.

TRUBY: [*alarmed*] What are you doing?

RUMMEL: The condemned dolphin ate a hearty meal.

RUMMEL throws fish in the air all over the place into TWO's tank. TWO leaps and snaps them—the fastest we have seen him move, and there is nothing wrong with his appetite.

WATCHERS are fascinated, pointing.

Now RUMMEL goes and gets a brightly-colored beach ball—a real one, not imaginary.

TRUBY: *[agitated]* What are you doing?

RUMMEL: *[bouncing the ball for punctuation and emphasis]* Sensory invariety, sensory deprivation. Same old same old same old same old. And in isolation. I say to Bamberger, why not make a channel between the tanks, so the two of them can get together after work. Dolphins are social. He says, 'Not in my experimental design. Not on my grant. Not in my lab.' So I say, why not let them have something to play with, after work, at night. Something real simple, like a beach ball. He says they won't give it back, they won't want to work. I talk him into trying it. And sure enough—One brings hers back, she'll do anything for the fish. Two, though—he won't bring his back, and he won't work, and Bamberger's out a day of his precious time. Grissom puts up signs, No Toys. Here a sign, there a sign, everywhere a sign—I go to the john, there's a No Toys sign floating in the bowl. I say to Bamberger—next time the great man is here, gracing us with his presence—instead of rationing him to just one ball, why not put in a dozen balls, a hundred, a dump truck. Satiate him, he'll get tired of them. A buck fifty a ball—cost-efficient, time-efficient. And Bamberger says, 'No, the more we put in, the more we have to get out.' I say, well, just one ball, then, and Bamberger says, 'If we let him have a ball, it's only going to be frustrating to him when we take it away. If we don't let him have a ball in the first place, there's no frustration.' There's no frustration? There are none so blind as those who will not see, and Bamberger, man, he qualifies for the No-See Hall of Fame. The Bamberger statue, the great man in symbolic pose—standing on the mountaintop, reaching for the future, eyes on the prize, head up the ass.

RUMMEL moves to roll the ball into TWO's tank.

TRUBY tries to stop him.

RUMMEL fakes him out and rolls the ball in.

TWO can't believe it. He startles, quivers with delight, then goes after the ball, playing with it, rolling it around, chasing it and catching it, balancing it—a hundred things you can do with a beach ball if you're a dolphin.

WATCHERS jump up, gasping.

TRUBY instantly turns his back on the tank, speaks as if to WATCHERS and audience.

TRUBY: I dissociate myself from this. *[loudly, into recorder]*
I disassociate myself. Emphatically. Utterly.

> *RUMMEL has gone to an imaginary phone and is
> making silent calls. As he does, party music fades in.*

11. PARTY

Night.

Party music gets louder.

*WATCHERS respond to RUMMEL's phone calls in
speech fragments, and begin to arrive at TWO's tank
for a party, as FRIENDS OF RUMMEL.*

*TRUBY backs off, all the way to the far side of ONE's
tank, where he sits by himself, watching, talking silently into his recorder.*

—Hey!

—What's up?

—Wanna come down to the lab?

—Who's gonna be there?

—Just us and the dolphins.

—You up for tonight?

—Yeah. What's on?

—Swim time.

—Whooee.

FRIENDS are now gathered tankside.

RUMMEL: Don't dive-bomb. It's their space. They've got to invite you in. Just hang your leg down and wait and see—

RUMMEL goes in first. Then one by one, FRIENDS slip into TWO's tank.

—Oogh. It's cold.

TWO is delighted, and shows it physically. This is by far the freest movement we have seen from him.

—It's OK to swim with him?

—Check him out. He'll let you know.

RUMMEL: Tuck your head in tight against his head, and you can zip around real fast.

—When he echo-locates, you can feel it—

—Right through you—

—To the marrow—

—You can really feel it.

—And he's whistling!

> *Good times are had by all, the humans throwing the beach ball around, catching rides with TWO.*

—And she would let herself go, right down to the bottom, and just be lying there, blowing bubbles, watch them float up.

—Great bubbles.

—Balloons of light. And sometimes she would follow them up, and just guide them with her beak, spin them.

—So delicate.

—Never burst them.

—And other times she would burst them around me, into thousands of bubbles, I'd be swimming through this storm of bubbles.

—Immaculate surf, six feet, breaking left.

—And this dolphin in the curl, right beside me.

—In and out of the wave, in, out, in, out, a flash, like a sailmaker's needle—

—Whooee—

—I stayed in with him, two hours—

—I got tired before he did . . .

—He kept holding my arm, under his pec.

—Wouldn't let go . . . He wanted company . . .

Party music starts a slow fade.

Party ends with FRIENDS leaving tank. They walk away from TWO's tank, talking among themselves, then turn back into WATCHERS.

TWO and RUMMEL are still in the tank, playing with the beach ball. RUMMEL leaves the ball with TWO and gets out.

He starts over to where TRUBY has been looking on. Along the way he stoops, and comes up with another beach ball.

Party music fades to silence.

12. A TRAINING PROBLEM,
A TRAINING SOLUTION

Straight on.

RUMMEL stands in front of TRUBY, who sits hunched, as if he has been slugged in the solar plexus, appalled at the unprofessionalism he has witnessed.

RUMMEL: You were invited.

TRUBY doesn't answer. RUMMEL bounces the beach ball in front of him.

RUMMEL: You've never swum with one, have you?

TRUBY still doesn't answer, silent, lips tight. Suddenly he sneezes, a huge sneeze, an 11 on a scale of 10.

RUMMEL: Good one, Truby. If you held that one back, you would have blowed it out your toes. Yeah, free your blowhole and your heart and mind will surely follow.

TRUBY: *[as soon as he can speak]* I dissociate myself—

RUMMEL turns and rolls the beach ball into ONE's tank.

TRUBY: *[leaping to his feet]* NO-O-O!

ONE, who has been circling, startles at the sight of the ball, then comes toward it from the edge of the tank, noses it curiously, then takes it to the edge of the tank and starts circling, pushing it ahead of her.

RUMMEL: Dissociate yourself from that.

TRUBY: *[following ONE]* No, no, no, no—

He follows her around the tank, no-no-no-ing in crescendo.

RUMMEL puts a hand to TRUBY's chest and stops him.

TRUBY points at RUMMEL straightarmed, as if he wishes he was holding a pistol.

TRUBY: Don't touch me, Rummel, you unprofessional son of a bitch. Keep your hands off. You've done it to me.

I don't care what damage you do to yourself and your damn delinquent dolphin, but don't you dare do it to me. What is Grissom going to say when he comes in and finds the ball—

RUMMEL: Truby, Truby, Truby. Observe yourself. Stereotyped behavior. It's not the end of the world. Think of it as a challenge. Another training exercise.

TRUBY: What do you mean?

RUMMEL: Think, Truby. One is fish-driven. She will do anything for fish. She's got the ball, you've got fish. Give her fish, she'll give you the ball.

> *TRUBY considers. Then he goes and gets a bucket of fish.*
>
> *ONE is still swimming in her stereotyped counter-clockwise direction, pushing the ball.*
>
> *TRUBY stands ahead of her, throws a first fish, short of her. ONE takes it and goes back to pushing the ball. TRUBY throws another, shorter, and another. Success. ONE comes closer each time, pushing the ball, without having to veer from her stereotyped route.*
>
> *Speech fragments from WATCHERS.*

—A new behavior can normally be shaped—

—In something like—

—Sixteen to twenty—

—Successive approximations.

—*[overlapping]* Successive approximations.

—If one shaping procedure is not progressing, go to another.

—There are as many ways of producing behaviors as there are trainers.

RUMMEL: OK now, this is for the gold medal.

He takes a fish and throws it behind ONE, so she has to reverse to catch it. This separates her from the ball. She swims quickly to retrieve the ball and resumes her counterclockwise swimming. RUMMEL throws another fish behind her. Same thing.

Then RUMMEL walks with the fish bucket far behind ONE, so she has to turn around to see him. He throws another fish. ONE goes after it—and she is facing in the opposite direction. She turns back to get the ball, then turns with it, facing where the fish are coming from. If she swims, now she will be swimming clockwise—a revolution in her behavior.

RUMMEL: All yours, Truby. Go get 'em, big guy.

TRUBY walks with the bucket as far away from ONE as possible in the clockwise direction. From there, throw by throw, he brings ONE to him—just as earlier he learned to bring her successfully to the bite bar.

Between fish, ONE is pushing the ball ahead of her—closer and closer to TRUBY.

Finally, tensely, ONE is close enough for TRUBY to reach down and take the ball—if she will let him. It is like the moment when he solo-trained ONE to accept the bite bar for the first time.

—If you can end the session on a high note, good.

With one hand TRUBY holds up a fish. ONE must rise to take it. As she does, TRUBY with his other hand scoops up the ball.

—Be sure to quit while you're ahead.

TRUBY looks at RUMMEL. RUMMEL throws him a fish.

RUMMEL: Free your mind, and the dolphin will follow.

TRUBY walks away to stash the ball and the fish bucket.

Right then, GRISSOM comes striding in, by TWO's tank—

And sees TWO playing with a ball—

13. GRISSOM TAKES A FALL

Straight on.

GRISSOM: What in the aquamarine blue blazes is that ball doin' in there? Of all days—

RUMMEL: Must have washed up with the tide.

GRISSOM: Tide? What tide? What are you talkin' about, Rummel?

RUMMEL: Or the wind blew it in. The wayward wind.

GRISSOM: What are you on? It's from your loonie tunes satiation number, isn't it? Dejà balls. You brought 'em in, unauthorized, and Bamberger thumbed you down, and you didn't get rid of 'em, you threw 'em in with the rest of your junk, that rat's nest, and you didn't secure 'em.

Rummel, I swear, it's like you've got helium in your head.

RUMMEL gives a shamefaced-looking shrug.

GRISSOM: *[continuing]* We're gonna have to adjust your attitude. Well, don't just stand there. Get the damn ball out. You know what Bamberger says about variables. Especially in the tanks. You know what he wants. Today onwards, extra sessions. You know what I've got to get through. I flat don't have *time*—

RUMMEL: *[sincerely apologetic]* It's just—Two's got me stymied, Grissom. You saw what he was doing to me yesterday. Maybe it *is* me. I never would have thought it, I don't *like* to think it. But maybe it is. A training problem—

GRISSOM: Train*er* problem, how I see it.

RUMMEL: OK, so I'm the problem. You could be the solution. Like Dr. Bamberger says: 'If there's a training problem, there's a training solution.' So how about you give it a try? I mean, you've got the experience, you've done the repetitions.

GRISSOM: You got that right. Anything's better than you and your helium-head amateur night Rummeltalk. Fetch me the bucket, I'll get this show on the road.

RUMMEL trots away dutifully and comes back with a

bucket of frozen smelt, which he hands to GRISSOM.

TRUBY is watching intently from ONE's tank, with his recorder.

GRISSOM shapes up, with TWO at the far side of the tank from him.

WATCHERS show great interest. Speech fragments.

—A new behavior can usually be shaped—

—[*overlapping*] In something like—

—[*overlapping*] Sixteen to twenty—

—[*overlapping*] Successive approximations—

GRISSOM begins throwing fish to bring TWO closer with the ball.

—Twenty.

—Nineteen.

—Eighteen.

—Seventeen.

—Sixteen.

TWO is complacently snapping up fish, coming closer with the ball. GRISSOM is looking good.

GRISSOM: *[to Rummel]* See, Rummel—this is why I get the big bucks.

—Fifteen.

—Fourteen.

—Thirteen.

GRISSOM: Yessir, old age and cunning will prevail over helium-heads and blowholes—

—Twelve.

GRISSOM:—Every time.

—Eleven.

—Ten.

TWO cruises right in to the edge of the tank, and GRISSOM leans down to grab the ball.

GRISSOM: *[intense, low voice]* Got it! Get some!

But at the last millisecond, TWO veers away and backs off into the center of the tank with the ball.

RUMMEL: Oh, tough—

GRISSOM: Who moved? Who moved? Can I have concentration? Huh?

RUMMEL: We're with you, Grissom. Behind you all the way. Go, team.

—Nine.

—Eight.

And once again TWO is coming closer.

—Seven.

—Six.

—Five.

—Four.

From here, WATCHERS count in unison.

ALL: Three . . . Two . . . One.

Again TWO is close enough for GRISSOM to reach down for the ball.

TWO moves tantalizingly back and forth, making GRISSOM mirror his movements. Then TWO offers the ball, but in the last millisecond and at the last millimeter, he pulls back, and—

GRISSOM overreaches and topples into the tank.

Before he can come up for air, TWO has scooted all the way back to the far side, with the ball.

Uproarious laughter from WATCHERS.

GRISSOM, wringing wet, is helped up onto the platform by RUMMEL, to speech fragments from WATCHERS.

—Out he came.

—And in he went.

—You should have been there!

—You should have seen him!

—Grissom.

—Grissom the Great.

—Striding out with the official green bucket.

—And he sets himself.

—Grissom the top gun.

—Fastest gun in the lab.

—He sets himself.

—He quick-draws a frozen smelt.

—And he shoots himself in the foot!

—Twenty fish, twenty repetitions.

—Twenty successive approximations.

—Dolphins 20, Grissom 0.

—Dolphins all the way.

—Two's game.

—Twenty fish.

—He trained Grissom to give him twenty fish!

> GRISSOM *doesn't want to look* RUMMEL *in the eye.*
> *He seizes on* TRUBY *to shout at.*

GRISSOM: What are you gapin' at, Truby? Standin' there, mouth hangin' open like a fish bucket. You've got an animal. We've got a grant renewal here, hangin' on productivity. So produce. Do some *science*. While I get this—I don't know what the hell this is over here—Lord knows it ain't science, it's some—twisted—crazed—rock and roll whatever—

TRUBY goes to the console and calls ONE to the bite bar.

Through the following we see TRUBY gesturing, ONE doing repetitions, and from ONE's tank we hear electronic tones at low volume, background noise level.

GRISSOM: *[to RUMMEL]* Get the ball out of there.

RUMMEL shrugs—how?

GRISSOM: *[continuing]* Drain the tank.

RUMMEL: Strand him again? We only just—

GRISSOM: Drain the tank. Get the ball out of there.

RUMMEL:—It's not good husbandry.

GRISSOM points. RUMMEL makes no move.

RUMMEL: *[continuing]* Grissom, in the wild they strand themselves to die, you know that.

GRISSOM: You're the one cracked this bad oyster open, Rummel, you get to eat it.

GRISSOM strides to the drain valve, opens it, then heads off to the ladder.

RUMMEL throws up his arms, and goes to sit on the platform.

For a bit, he watches TWO. Then he chirrups. TWO comes over with the ball and noses up at him.

RUMMEL speaks to WATCHERS and indirectly to the audience, as he did in his training demonstrations. WATCHERS interpolate.

RUMMEL: They're not fish, they're mammals. Warm-blooded. Big-brained. The brain of *Tursiops truncatus montagu* is bigger than the brain of *Homo sapiens*. His brain—*[touching TWO's head]*—is bigger than my brain, bigger than yours, bigger than Grissom's. And the neo-cortical area of his brain—

—Is bigger than in the human brain.

—Not only in relation to total brain size—

—But in absolute size.

RUMMEL: His neocortex is bigger than my neocortex, your neocortex. And the significance of that is—

—The neocortical area—

—After motor response and sensory response areas in the brain are mapped—

—In humans—

RUMMEL:—Everything that makes us human, that distinguishes us as human, originates and resides in the neocortical area of the brain—

—Memory and desire—

—The ability to look back and look forward—

—Planning—

—And the dolphin brain—

—Has more neocortical area than the human brain—

—Both in absolute terms—

—And relative to total brain size—

RUMMEL: Regionally differentiated—

—Elaborate—

—Highly convoluted—

RUMMEL: . . . Why shouldn't there be a mind in there?

> *TRUBY has come over to the platform beside RUM-*
> *MEL. He speaks not to RUMMEL, but to WATCH-*
> *ERS and audience.*

TRUBY: Which is precisely the fascination. To find out what that big brain can do compared with ours. What we can do with it.

—Everything that defines us as human—

TRUBY: To crack the code of dolphin echo-location. We are looking to make use of the ocean. These animals can work for us—

—The ability to abstract—

—To symbolize—

—A moral sense, an ethical sense—

—Everything that makes us human—

—Is in the neocortex.

RUMMEL: And he has more neocortex than I have . . .
Than you have . . . Than Bamberger has . . . Than even
Truby has . . . So where do you draw the line? Where do
I draw the line?

TRUBY: [*turning to RUMMEL, indicating water level*]
Black line.

> RUMMEL *and* WATCHERS *move into the tank, and*
> *push and shove* TWO *to center tank, where he is*
> *stranded—as in the tank-cleaning scene earlier, hang-*
> *ing on the trapeze like a side of meat.*

TRUBY: [*in audience-addressing mode*] Take the broad view,
the long view, the high ground. A few individual animals—set them in the balance against the whole weight
of scientific progress, human progress. What do they
amount to, what do they signify? And even for those few
individual animals—sure, they have to work, but so do I.
They are fed, they are safe. They gain, we gain. It's a fair
contract.

> WATCHERS *are withdrawing from the tank, listening*
> *as they go.*

> RUMMEL *has climbed out of the tank, right below*
> TRUBY.

RUMMEL: Two signed the contract? With an underwater ballpoint? When he was caught, did they read him his rights?

TRUBY: [*not responding, still in audience-addressing mode*] If we are going make the ocean productive—how these animals communicate—

RUMMEL: Communicate. Of course they communicate. Ants communicate. But what if dolphins have language?

Longish pause.

TRUBY turns to RUMMEL, and from now on they speak directly to each other.

TRUBY: Do you mean a language of their own? Some kind of Dolphinese? Or do you mean potentiality for human language? Debatable either way, Rummel— whether any animal—not just this species—has true language potentiality, much less capability. Endlessly debated. Of course they communicate among themselves. But even on the remote chance that these animals do have what we might—at a stretch—call a true language of their own, it would be species-specific.

RUMMEL: You mean like, 'If a lion could speak, we could not understand what it was saying.' Wittgenstein.

TRUBY: Who?

RUMMEL: Wittgenstein. Remedial Philosophy 101.

TRUBY: *[with recorder]* How do you spell that?

RUMMEL: P-H-

TRUBY: No, Rummel—Wittgenstein.

RUMMEL: W-I-T-T-G-E-N—

TRUBY:—S-T-E-I-N. Of course. I knew that.

RUMMEL: But what if—what if? I don't mean this—*[doing experiment gestures]*—a human command language, an imposed language, the dolphins do what they're told or they don't get to eat, and everything they learn comes down to how to score a stinking dead fish. I mean both sides using linguistic symbols that have an agreed meaning—

Another longish pause.

TRUBY: Rummel, you're being extraordinarily matter-of-fact about an amazing accretion and concatenation of untenable suppositions.

He jumps down into the tank and heads for the beach ball.

RUMMEL: But what if—what if—a dolphin could speak to us in a way we could understand? What would we have done? Would we have taught an animal to speak? Or would we have liberated a human being? Kafka. K-A-F-K-A.

TRUBY scoops up the ball and throws it in the air and catches it as he speaks.

TRUBY: Aha—aha—do I detect the surfacing of an agenda? Captive research is politically incorrect—is that what you're implying? Is that what this all about? Then why won't you just come out and say it? Dr. Bamberger—if there's one thing he has always stood for, always championed, it is scientific research as value-free. He stands scrupulously aside from politics, in favor of the scientifically correct—and I stand with him.

RUMMEL: But think about it. If they could speak, and we could understand, what would they be saying?—*[to WATCHERS]*—There's this chimp—*[to TRUBY]*—as you may or may not know, you being the pigeon person that you are—*[back to WATCHERS]*—and the chimp brain is only a quarter the size of Truby's, a fifth the size of Two's—and this chimp is one of the ones they taught sign language, ASL, American Sign Language. Built him up to a vocabulary of five hundred words. Nouns, verbs, adjectives, names—and he responded—

TRUBY: All that is trainable. It is perfectly well explained in terms of stimulus and response. You don't have to inflate it, pump it up to anything more than that. It does-n't *entail* language—

RUMMEL: *[still to WATCHERS]* —Then up to phrases, to sentences. Initiating as well as responding, productive as well as receptive. He started signing new sentences, com-bining known words in new ways. New *thoughts*—*[mak-ing sign language signs]*—They had him take an IQ test, customized for chimps, but all the human categories, everything. To the national standard. Scored 90-plus. Qualified him at least for a football scholarship—he could be getting bids from community colleges in Southern California . . . So—this lab has had the chimp for years, from when he was taken away from his moth-er. This day, he's put in his hours, he's done his repeti-tions, he's got his food reward. The principal scientist, the grantmaster, is locking him in and taking off, and the chimp rattles the cage, looks at him through the bars, and signs—*[signing]*—'Me Out, You In' . . . You don't think that qualifies as a political statement?

TRUBY: Why does everything with you always come down to funny stories? This is serious business. Of course there are costs to the animal. But look at the rewards, for heaven's sake, the benefits to humanity. There's no com-parison. Rummel—you make me giddy. You can come on with your chimp hahas and your Kissinger hohos, and you can quote Kafka and spell W-I-T-T-genstein all you want, and all you're doing is spinning your wheels, and no one is any farther forward. And then this misbegotten—you drive the whole bus off the cliff—and you don't care who you take down with you. Well, if you're not going to lead and you're not going to follow, get out of the way.

He climbs out of the tank with the beach ball, just about jostling RUMMEL. Angrily, he spins the wheel of the drain valve to close it, and plants himself right beside it, sitting on the beach ball, a guardian.

Electronic music starts.

RUMMEL watches the water rise.

TWO moves, almost able to swim.

RUMMEL climbs down into the tank to swing TWO free, out of the holding tank.

As he moves back and up out of the tank, electronic music rises higher.

14. DOLPHIN DANCE

Straight on.

ONE in her tank does not dance, she just porpoises, in alternating directions, not stereotyped, yet not really free in movement.

But TWO, as soon as he has full motion, goes crazy.

Electronic music escalates.

TWO slams around in a rage, leaping and smacking down, every which way, in a frenzy.

WATCHERS jump to their feet and stare, their eyes bugging out.

TRUBY stands up and backs away from the tank, almost tripping over the beach ball. He takes out his recorder, raises it to his mouth, then lowers it.

RUMMEL covers his eyes with his hands and bends his head.

TWO halts for a moment, beak darting back and forth, then starts attacking the wall of the tank, making repeated high-speed assaults, as if he is trying to batter his way out. Failing there, he turns to a second part of the wall. Failing there, to a third. And at his first smash here, the electronic music abruptly cuts out, as if TWO has destroyed the hydrophone that picks up tank sounds.

RUMMEL looks up, and—into the silence comes GRISSOM, down the ladder, trailing a long trail of fax paper.

He strides to the platform.

GRISSOM: They—ain't—renewin'—the—grant.

He draws his foot back to deliver a vicious kick at the beach ball.

ALL freeze, including TWO and ONE.

And as GRISSOM launches his kick—blackout.

ACT TWO

1. THE LAB IS SHUT DOWN

Day.

The loudspeaker is lying on the floor, horn down. Beside it are the two consoles, one standing, the other turned over on its side.

The main divide between the tanks is gone, but everyone behaves as if it is still there, and we should imagine that it is. The wooden platform remains.

ONE and TWO are swimming separately on each side of the imagined divide. As always, they give no sign that they are aware of each other's existence. ONE no longer moves in stereotyped fashion.

GRISSOM and TRUBY are tensely studying a very, very long fax—many feet long.

WATCHERS are studying a similar fax, one copy between them, the long sheet passing through their hands as if it is going down an assembly line.

CELESTE is sitting apart, off to one side of the action, wearing a designer version of the standard costume. She is meditating: full lotus, eyes closed, hands stylishly in a mudra position.

RUMMEL is standing on the platform.

When he speaks, WATCHERS pay attention. GRISSOM and TRUBY do not; they keep studying the long fax, GRISSOM hogging it, reading slowly, moving his lips, TRUBY impatient to get at it, scanning rapidly, speaking silently into his recorder. And CELESTE keeps meditating.

RUMMEL: One never knows, do one? Satchel Paige. No—Fats Waller? One of those great philosophers . . . There's a funny story—Truby doesn't like funny stories, so call it a parable. This guy's in business for himself. Fast-tracking, got everything going for him. Heavy hitter with a hot hand, yes, he's going to have it all, top of the heap, A-Number One, up where he belongs, and he knows he deserves it—all that good stuff. Big new car, black Cadillac, both hands on the wheel and his shoulders thrown back, and away in the back there's money in a sack. Roger Miller. So—his cell phone rings. He picks up. 'Swinging Dick Enterprises, this is Swinging Dick.' And a digital voice says—*[very fast from here]*—'Hi, Mr. Dick, this is Loretta, from Fairy Godmothers New Improved Three Wishes, as advertised on TV, not available in stores. To introduce our unique product, you have been selected to participate in a special exclusive offer. One instant free wish. Limited time only, while stocks last, never to be repeated. To make a wish, press Star. If you're one of those dorks that can't make up your mind, press D-O-R-K and an operator will assist you. Wishes processed in order received.' 'Me first,' says Dick, in his confident not-to-be-denied executive-suite decision-making deep baritone. 'I want that my swinging, ahem, equipment should touch the floor.' And the fairy godmother voice says, 'To confirm and fulfill your wish, press Star,' and he does, and there's this electronic blip, and a disconnect buzz, and he looks down, and he's cut off at the hips . . .

Pause.

TRUBY: [*studying fax, to GRISSOM*] They've been declared *surplus? Excess to needs?* I can't believe it.

GRISSOM: Read it and weep. One big moose research cutback, system-wide. One big mother marine mammal cutback. Meaning one Big Mary job cutback. A real kick in the gonads, which are near and dear to my heart. I— am—hurtin'.

TRUBY: And we're cut? They're shutting down the lab?

GRISSOM: One big moose mother Mary mothball.

TRUBY: So what's this 'facility' they're sending the animals—

GRISSOM: Goin' to be like one big marine mammal

warehouse. B-i-g dolphin storage locker. They're inventoryin' the surplus, nationwide. Animals from all the programs that didn't make the cut under the new guidelines, didn't get budgeted. Goin' to be bringin' em in from everywhere.

TRUBY: What about jobs there, then? There'll be more animals than anywhere else.

RUMMEL: [to WATCHERS] More captive dolphins than any place in history, ever. How about that?

TRUBY: [to GRISSOM] Think of the research opportunities—

GRISSOM: [to TRUBY] No research. No trainin'. No nothin'. Personnel for maintenance. Keep 'em fed, minimum rations, minimum wage work—Rummel level—and that's all she wrote.

TRUBY: Have you seen the place?

GRISSOM: Was there once with Bamberger. It's holdin' pens. Thirty by thirty foot each. Right in the harbor. They're gonna have to build more—no end of pens.

RUMMEL: [to WATCHERS] That harbor. The water's toxic. Fall in, you don't drown, you dissolve. [to TWO] What do you say, Two—let's bail for Tahiti, throw in with pearl divers or something.

TRUBY: [to GRISSOM, *shuffling fax*] I don't understand—there's no provision for me. Rummel, I can see why—of course not. But me—I can't believe Dr. Bamberger—

RUMMEL: [*to TRUBY*] It was a fair contract, wasn't it? You signed, you made your mark. You worked, you got rewarded. Advancing science for the good of humanity, that was your reward. That was then, this is now. Bamberger does his new sums—the shark must keep moving forward or it dies. Either you're a line item in his budget or you're not, and you're not. You're surplus. You used to be science, now you're history.

TRUBY: But my contract isn't up. I'm owed—I'm entitled—

GRISSOM: Here's a quarter, call someone who cares.

RUMMEL: Travis Tritt. Put not thy trust in princes. Psalm 146, Verse 3.

TRUBY: [*rounding on RUMMEL*] Rummel, you know as well as I do what did it. It was that—chaos with Two. And you're responsible. You're the one. You put the ball in the tank. Look at you—you trash my career, you reduce everything around you to wreckage, and you squat grinning in the rubble, and you have the gall to be citing Scripture to your own purpose. You make me giddy.

> GRISSOM *has spotted something of great interest to him in the fax. He tears that one page out of the middle of the long strip of fax paper, drops the rest, and heads for the ladder.*

TRUBY sees this. Panicked about being left out of the information loop, he takes off after GRISSOM.

TRUBY: Grissom, wait—

WATCHERS scrabble to locate this page on their copy of the fax.

As TRUBY and GRISSOM go, WATCHERS read aloud from their fax sheets.

—For surplus animals—

—The options to be evaluated are—

—Euthanasia—

—Unviable—

—Politically undesirable—

—For community relations reasons—

RUMMEL: Had me going there for a moment.

—Status quo—

—The animal stays at the facility in which it has been housed—

RUMMEL: Out. Bamberger didn't get his grant renewed—Bloody Friday.

—Translocation—

—The animal is moved to a facility other than the one where it has been maintained—

RUMMEL: The holding pens. Up to the blowhole in the Big Filthy. Maximum security. Alcatraz and water.

2. CELESTE APPEARS, RADIATING LIGHT

Straight on.

CELESTE has been continuing to meditate, eyes downcast, the perfection of her posture marred only by the fact that, often enough to be noticeable—three times, say—she disengages one hand from her mudra and scratches her head or touches her closed eyelid or dabs at the tip of her tongue. The fingers of the moving hand, however, remain in a perfect mudra, and she makes a special little performance of returning the hand super-meticulously to meditating position, followed by a little self-aware shoulder-settling shrug.

—Option Four—

—To place carefully selected surplus animals in carefully

selected amusement parks, on a contract basis, with a royalty to be levied on revenues earned by the park.

RUMMEL: *[to WATCHERS]* Amusement parks, abusement parks. Petting pools. Teeth filed down to the nub, kids sticking quarters in their blowholes. And showtime, coming right up, folks, on the hour every hour. See the fearless trainer dominate the mighty dolphin. Some college dropout, lord of creation in a tanktop. Always the human on top. Why is that? What if it was the other way around? How would that be? . . . Ha—minks in old Miami lady skin coats . . . A big old bear, he's watching TV, drinking Red Dog out of the can, and over the fireplace he's got this stuffed guy in an orange vest with a gun . . . You and your girlfriend, you're making love on the lawn, and this uptight redneck pit bull comes charging out of the house and turns the hose on you . . .

CELESTE opens her eyes and holds out both hands, palms up, toward RUMMEL—a gesture signifying Spirituality.

CELESTE: But it doesn't have to be that way—surely not between we and the dolphins. Humankind and dolphinkind are one. If we nurture dolphins, they will nurture us in return, manyfold.

CELESTE is one of those people who can come straight up out of a full lotus, no hands. She does, and walks toward RUMMEL, still with her hands out.

CELESTE: *[continuing]* So simple, so beautiful. And it came to me so unexpectedly— *[She writes in the air, fingers once again in the mudra position.]* —'Life is a gift. All the rest is shopping.' Enlightenment! And of all times and places, when I was trying on this very wet suit. Naked in a fitting room on Rodeo Drive, and it changed my life. Synchronicity. In that instant I knew—I *knew*—what my mission was to be—to create—*[writing in the air again]*— The Sign Of The Dolphin.

RUMMEL: *[to WATCHERS]* 'I am writing my autobiography and I would appreciate hearing from anyone who can remember anything interesting or exciting about my life. Signed, Your friend—'

CELESTE comes to a halt in front of RUMMEL.

CELESTE: I am Celeste.

RUMMEL: Celeste.

CELESTE: —My mission statement—To bring together dolphins who urgently need a loving home, and children who desperately need hope . . . physically challenged, autistic . . . Bring them together in . . . swim therapy. A win-win situation.

RUMMEL: A win, as we say, win situation. Swim therapy. In amusement parks.

CELESTE: *[to WATCHERS]* Where better to spread the word, how better to spread the joy? Millions of human beings every year, responding to the precious gift the dolphins offer us. The gift of nurturing.

RUMMEL: So dolphins are nurturing—

CELESTE: And altruistic. They are not selfish, they care for each other. They care for their own dying loved ones. And they care for us. Those heartwarming stories—so many of them—fully authentic—of course you've seen them on TV—drowning humans brought back to shore— back to life—saved by dolphins.

Now, while RUMMEL speaks, CELESTE begins circling the tanks, looking at ONE and TWO.

RUMMEL: *[to WATCHERS]* Dolphins have a pushing behavior. They push things. They'll do it in the tank— beach ball, boogie board, styrofoam cup, anything interesting. Every so often in the wild, the interesting thing is a human. They may well push the interesting human in to shore. Or they may well push him, or as the case may be, her—*[indicating CELESTE]*—out to sea and gone. Of humans who report being pushed by dolphins, one hundred percent have been pushed in to shore. Humans pushed out to sea, now—the percentage of them reporting in is considerably lower, like zero.

CELESTE: *[shaking her head forgivingly]* That's so—heartless of you. So—un-dolphinesque. Dolphins are aware of our inner states of being.

RUMMEL: *[to WATCHERS]* This is the one about them echo-locating on your body, sonaring your soft tissue, checking out your insides—hence your internal emotional state—hence the state of your soul.

CELESTE: If you had ever swum with a dolphin, you would have felt it for yourself. Or else you are totally unfeeling.

RUMMEL: Uh-huh. And you've been swimming with them—

CELESTE: Three months now.

RUMMEL: Wow.

CELESTE: And it feels like forever—I trust it *will* be forever. That pulse. Pure communication. No barriers. So intimate. After all, the human heart is soft tissue. *[CELESTE has begun gravitating towards TWO's tank.]* I have been blessed with the gift of affinity. To me, as a caring human being, to withhold my gift would be heartless. So, I have made a commitment. For the sake of the children. For the sake of the dolphins.

She sits on the edge of TWO's tank, dangling her legs. TWO comes nosing up to her. She extends a leg. TWO bobs around it, close but never touching it.

CELESTE: *[continuing]* Dr. Bamberger—I acknowledge his brilliance—I and he are not souls in harmony—but, as I said to him—and I could *sense* him sincerely questing after my meaning—ultimately we are all pilgrims, on the same path. He—and others like him, at this emotional moment in time for the dolphins—I was able to get them to sit down, around the table with a consortium of the most prestigious parks, and I offered to be the one to—

RUMMEL: Audition the dolphins—?

CELESTE:—Sense where the affinities are closest and warmest. So that the program can be the best it can be. For the sake of the children, for the sake of the dolphins . . . I sense something here. It resonates with me.

She slips into TWO's tank.

3. CELESTE HAS AN UNFORTUNATE EXPERIENCE

Straight on.

TWO moves his head around, sonaring CELESTE. She gives a pleasurable little "ah." Then a somewhat more agitated "oh."

RUMMEL: *[to WATCHERS]* One thing they're very interested in is sonaring, how shall we say, in academic language, genitalia.

Without further ceremony, TWO pounces on CELESTE and embarks upon what looks like attempted rape.

WATCHERS react, but do nothing. RUMMEL looks on dispassionately.

A terrible commotion in the tank. TWO is all over CELESTE, especially with his head. It looks as if he is trying to tear her wet suit off.

RUMMEL: *[to WATCHERS, as CELESTE struggles]* There's a scientific explanation. When dolphins sonar you, they are—true enough—looking into your soft tissue. They sonar everything underwater—turtles, manatees, Coke bottles. It's how they identify things: shape, size, what kind of stuff it's made of, how fast it's moving—what's up, what are the happenings? A wet suit interferes with that. Neoprene has air cells that look very 'bright' to dolphin sonar. Penetration is limited. Now, dolphins are curious. Here's this interesting new thing in the tank. It's alive, but what is it? So the dolphin tries to take the wet suit off you . . . Purely, you understand, in the interests of marine mammal science: the never-ending dolphin quest for knowledge.

CELESTE is halfway to hysteria. Eventually she struggles free, fending TWO off with her foot, floundering toward the edge of the tank.

TWO lounges to center tank and lolls around there.

RUMMEL: *[To WATCHERS]* That's Scientific Explanation Number One. Scientific Explanation Number Two would be—sex and the single dolphin. Two doesn't get to, how shall we say, date. It's not in Bamberger's protocol. So Two is, how shall we say, horny. Any chance he gets to rub up against something warm and moving, he'll jump it . . . Ha, old Two . . . Anyway, I suppose a swim therapy job is out of the question for him now—came on a tad too strong in the interview, didn't leave the right spiritual impression.

CELESTE is out of the tank, composing herself, taking off her mauled wet suit. She is wearing a bikini underneath.

CELESTE: Well . . . whew . . . quite . . . a . . . learning experience!

RUMMEL: *[indicating ONE]* On the other hand, Celeste, this one here—she's female. More sensitive, more receptive. None of those offensive male projectile erectile behaviors.

4. CELESTE HAS ANOTHER
UNFORTUNATE EXPERIENCE

Straight on.

RUMMEL walks over to ONE's tank, carrying the fish bucket; CELESTE follows.

He sits and dangles his legs into ONE's tank. With CELESTE watching, he makes a hand gesture we have not seen before, different from the experimental gestures. In response, ONE makes a movement we have not seen before. RUMMEL throws her a fish. This is repeated. Each of ONE's movements is very free, very engaging—and each is different from the last.

RUMMEL: *[to WATCHERS as well as CELESTE]* This is what we call 'novel behavior.' By the way, Celeste, you'll appreciate this—it was a female trainer who made the original discovery, with a female dolphin. So much training is grunt work, getting the dolphin to do the same thing over and over and over, years and years of it. But this trainer, she discovered that the dolphin wanted to play. More than that—dolphins have a genius for play . . . A conceptual breakthrough, a wonderful intuition. A great moment. She rewarded the dolphin every time it did something *different.* And the dolphin rewarded her with hundreds of new displays. No limit to the dolphin's inventiveness, even within the confines of the tank. Imagine what it would be like in the wild. *[to CELESTE now]* Just recently, we were serendipitously able to introduce this one to playtime. It's changed her life. Look.

He goes through the routine again. ONE is getting into it.

RUMMEL: *[continuing, explaining to CELESTE]* I'm sitting, not standing—that's the basic signal that it's playtime, she doesn't have to be grinding out work. And this is the signal for her to think of something new and playful.

He makes the playtime gesture again. ONE does a really nice unconstrained movement, more complex still, and looks up at RUMMEL as if to say, How's that? RUMMEL throws her a fish.

RUMMEL: *[continuing]* As long as you want to play, she will play. And every time she will show you something new.

He repeats his signal. ONE performs a totally different movement, free and complex. RUMMEL throws her a fish.

RUMMEL: *[continuing]* And she loves it if you finish off with a swim. In fact she expects it, she counts on it.

CELESTE: Can I—?

RUMMEL: You're sure you want to go in again?

CELESTE: Oh, of course. Learning experiences are learning experiences. I never stigmatize them as negative.

RUMMEL: Thrown from the horse, get back on again straight away. Good for you. There aren't many women game and groovy at the same time.

CELESTE: *[a bit archly]* I'm not 'many women.'

RUMMEL: No you're not. Sorry about the—ah—incident with the wet suit. Uh—just one, uh, small thing. The bikini. She's allergic to detergent. Even a trace. So feel free to take it off.

CELESTE gives him a look.

RUMMEL gets up and backs off a pace or two from the edge of the tank, out of her way, taking the fish bucket with him and setting it down directly behind her, out of sight of ONE.

CELESTE sits and dangles her legs.

ONE pays attention.

CELESTE makes the playtime hand signal.

ONE does an outstanding movement, the best yet, and looks up at CELESTE as if to say, How's that?

CELESTE applauds.

CELESTE: [to RUMMEL] Isn't that darling! [to ONE] Aren't you a charmer!

And with hands out to ONE, she slips into the tank for her swim.

Without ceremony, ONE immediately bustles CELESTE to the center of the tank, then straight down to the bottom, and lies on her, unmoving, heavy as a millstone. It looks like attempted drowning.

As when TWO was molesting CELESTE, WATCH-ERS react but do nothing.

RUMMEL [dispassionately, to WATCHERS] And the reason for this is—?

—The human did not positively reinforce—

—A correctly performed behavior—

—With the appropriate reward.

RUMMEL: And the dolphin is—

—Negatively reinforcing her.

RUMMEL: *[throwing WATCHERS a fish]* Correct.

CELESTE starts to show panic signs.

Whereupon ONE lets her up to breathe, then pushes her at speed straight to the edge of the tank, on the far side from RUMMEL. She climbs out shakily and flops down on her back, gasping for breath.

ONE keeps doing tail splashes and belly flops, trying to drive CELESTE farther away.

RUMMEL: *[to WATCHERS]* Marks on the left upper leg. All eighty-eight teeth.

CELESTE jolts upright, examines toothmarks, alarmed.

RUMMEL: *[continuing]* Never broke the skin, though. Negative reinforcement. For not positively reinforcing correct behavior. Exactly calibrated. Me, I always positively reinforce correct behavior. It's in my protocol.

He picks up the fish bucket, throws ONE a fish, and another, and another.

He gives WATCHERS fish to throw to ONE.

RUMMEL: *[continuing]* And the moral of the story is this. One is *fish-driven*. Don't ever get between One and the fish bucket. It's dangerous. The only thing I can think of more dangerous would be getting between Celeste and the six o'clock news camera.

During this, TRUBY has come halfway down the ladder and has been watching. Now he comes all the way down, walking toward CELESTE in sympathy.

TRUBY: *[to RUMMEL]* Why must you forever be tearing things down—look for the worst, do your worst? How can swim therapy be all bad?

RUMMEL: That sound—what might it be? Ah—it is the call of Truby, sonaring for work. The Truby Variations, on a theme of opportunism. 'I'm not cheap, but I'm on special this week.' Stephen Wright. Sending out the signal that swim therapy has redeeming social significance—

TRUBY: Come on now, Rummel.

RUMMEL: The park gives off a better ping than the pen.

TRUBY: Of course it's better.

RUMMEL: It's the difference between a Mexican jail and one of those upscale federal pens. They're both prisons.

TRUBY: Not a correct analogy. And you're making Celeste sound like the worst person in the world.

Now he is standing close to CELESTE.

RUMMEL: What—in the land of the total assholes, the half-assed one is king? Nah. She's halfway between attractive and ugly. I just wish she would be ugly altogether and get it over with—*[to WATCHERS now]*—The thing about therapy swims—as therapy, it's fine. But it doesn't take a dolphin. Do it with domesticated animals, dogs, horses. Do it with loving humans. Wonderful. The more the better. But you absolutely do not need captive dolphins . . . And in those parks it ain't about heart. It's about using dolphins for that good old heartwarming *image*. Figure it. You've got your showtime dolphins, they're making you X bucks an hour, ticket sales. You've got your swim-withs—rub up against an exotic creature, short time, big bucks. Huh—if it was humans, what would that be called? Now all of a sudden here comes this new socially redeeming thing. Biggest big bucks. Do your PR right, and you're on the TV tabloid shows. Right after the child-abuse head-shaker segment, you're the heartstring-tugger segment. You'll have parents lined up, you'll have to wait-list them, beat them off with a stick. And we're talking *significant* cash flow. For a course of therapy swims you can be charging a thousand bucks per disabled kid. That's got as much heart to it as a filtration pump. If they meant it, if they had heart, they'd be doing it for free.

He looks down at CELESTE. She is breathing heavily. looking up at him savagely.

RUMMEL: *[continuing]* And Celeste has the franchise. Sign Of The Dolphin, Inc. She's just talking the talk—putting her mouth where the money is.

CELESTE: *[jumping to her feet]* That's disgusting.

RUMMEL: Your choice of words.

CELESTE: *[her ultimate putdown]* You're not—an evolved consciousness.

And she wheels and stamps off, bumping into TRUBY, pushing him aside with distaste.

RUMMEL: *[to TRUBY]* An ugly end to an otherwise ugly occasion.

5. OPTIONS ARE EXPLORED

Straight on.

TRUBY: *[to RUMMEL]* You never stop, do you? Now

you've implicated me, contaminated me. No park is ever going to hire me—I'm from that place with the rapist murderer animals. What am I supposed to do now, Rummel? I was progressing exceptionally well, and now everything has turned to—I ask Grissom for advice and he just grunts. I call Dr. Bamberger and all I ever get is his machine, and he doesn't call back. It's a nightmare. Why did I ever come here? I was crazy.

RUMMEL: An impossible future imposed upon an ugly present in the shadow of the regretted past. Rummel.

TRUBY: Rummel!—

RUMMEL picks up the long fax that GRISSOM dropped, and hands it to TRUBY.

RUMMEL: Did you check Option Four?

WATCHERS shuffle their faxes, looking.

TRUBY: Of course I did. Controlled release. But that's all hypothetical. It's never going to happen. They spell it out in so many words.

WATCHERS read aloud from fax sheets.

—Just as proven methods of operant conditioning prepare animals for life in captivity—

—So proven methods of operant conditioning *could* be used to prepare them for reintroduction to the wild.

TRUBY: *[nodding]*— Sure, in theory training can go both ways. But—

—No compelling reason for reintroducing marine mammals into the wild.

—Further—

—Resources, methodologies and technologies for such projects do not currently exist.

TRUBY: *[to RUMMEL]* See?

—Development would take an estimated two years.

—Then five years of pilot studies.

—Actual reintroduction, monitoring and documentation another two to six years.

RUMMEL: And in the long run we'll all be dead. Keynes.

—Among all animals, only a few would qualify for reintroduction—

TRUBY: *[reading from fax]* —Depending on age, time in captivity, away from the wild. See, Rummel—One wouldn't make the cut anyway.

RUMMEL: Make that Two.

—A reintroduction project would not be cost-effective.

—Estimated costs are in the range from two to five times as expensive as maintaining the facility—

—The facility—

—The Option Five facility—

—Where surplus animals will be provided with the highest quality care for the duration of their lives.

—*[overlapping]* Highest quality care—

—*[overlapping]* For the duration of their lives.

RUMMEL: The plain English version—keep every one of them in a separate isolation pen, thirty foot by thirty, in toxic water, until they die.

—Why do they have to be penned?

—In isolation?

RUMMEL: They're trying to run the inventory down. Put them in together and they'll mate, they'll breed. You'll have more of them, not less. And for sure, in that harbor water—toxic heavy metals—you're going to get malformed births. Monstrous. You can just see that on the six o'clock news, it'd look like hidden camera footage from the Star Wars bar. *Bad* image day.

—Option Six—

—If the animals are not penned, it will be necessary to neuter them.

RUMMEL: Don't even think about that one. *[to TRUBY]* What would you think about Option Seven?

TRUBY: *[riffling fax paper to the end]* There is no Option Seven.

6. OPTION SEVEN

Straight on.

RUMMEL: Yes there is.

TRUBY: What?

RUMMEL: Release them anyway.

TRUBY: What? What??

RUMMEL: Release them anyway.

TRUBY: One and Two?

RUMMEL: Who else do you see here?

TRUBY: From here?

RUMMEL: Where else are we?

TRUBY: From here? Who—

RUMMEL: Who else do you see?

TRUBY: Us??

RUMMEL: Me and you. One and Two.

TRUBY flings the fax in the air.

TRUBY: Get away from me, Rummel! Don't come near me. You're dangerous. You're barking mad. Criminally insane.

Through the following, every time RUMMEL takes a step closer to him, TRUBY takes a countering step: evasive action.

RUMMEL: Think about it, Truby. They were going to die here in the tanks, however long it took. For science. Now they're going to die in the holding pens. Sooner. And not even for science. For nothing.

Pause.

TRUBY: But you can't just—

RUMMEL: Of course you can't 'just.' I wouldn't 'just.'

TRUBY: What would you do, then?—

RUMMEL: Check it out with them. Do they remember the ocean? Do they want to? Do they remember being dolphins with other dolphins? Do they want to? Do they remember how?

TRUBY: But the tanks aren't the ocean.

RUMMEL: Think oceanically, act locally. Start from where you are and go where you have to.

TRUBY: But—

RUMMEL: Start extinguishing captive behaviors, feed them up to wild weight and take it from there.

He grabs a fish bucket and starts throwing fish in the air, into the tanks, first TWO's tank, then ONE's.

RUMMEL: [*to the dolphins*] Go, go, go!

ONE and TWO are racing around, snapping fish out of the air.

RUMMEL races around, throwing.

WATCHERS jump up and join in, all throwing.

—Oh, she's fast—

—Look—

—Never misses—

—Wild weight—

—Wild dolphin—

—Born to hunt—

—Out of the tank—

—Over the wall—

—Wild dolphin—

—Hey, mackerel—

—A school—

—Two wild dolphins—

—Mackerel—

—Millions—

—The water's boiling with them—

—Born to hunt—

—Wild dolphins!

> *A WATCHER presses a bucket on TRUBY. He takes it and holds it a moment, but then rejects it, setting it down hard.*

> *This brings the throwing and feeding to an abrupt end.*

> *WATCHERS retreat.*

> *RUMMEL throws a last fish.*

RUMMEL: *[to WATCHERS]* For a moment there I thought I had him.

TRUBY: Rummel, Rummel. Listen to me. There's sharks out there. What chance do you give them against sharks? They've been captive for years.

RUMMEL: Ten years captivity, forty million years of evolution. And what hope do you give them anyway? In captivity, fifty percent deaths in seven years. You know that. And you know they're both on the wrong side of the time curve already. The captivity clock is ticking. And what hope do you give them in the pens? Heavy metals in the water, stress, all kinds of infections, pneumonia, gastroenteritis, septicemia—

TRUBY is making conflicted moaning sounds.

RUMMEL: *[continuing to WATCHERS]* And I almost thought I had him again. But—

TRUBY: Rummel, stop! You'd be acting without authority!

RUMMEL: Truby, you're full of fears. What if you were walking your chihuahua on the beach and a big pelican swooped down and snapped it up and flew off and there was only the leash hanging down?—What if you were walking in the woods and this big bear came along and took a dump and wiped its ass on your face?

TRUBY: Stop with your insane funny stories!

RUMMEL: That's what Big Bear Bamberger just did to you.

TRUBY: *THAT'S NOT FUNNY!*

He slumps and puts his heads in his hands.

RUMMEL: *[to WATCHERS]* And I really thought he was ready.

7. THE DANCE OF LIFE

Day turns to night as—

RUMMEL goes to where the two consoles have been stashed. He takes the console that was left standing, sets it up on a spot between the tanks, plugs it in, programs it, presses a switch—

And from the speaker in each tank comes a flood of open ocean sound.

ONE and TWO startle—they can't believe it.

Each rushes to a speaker, pressing right up against it, fairly vibrating with excitement.

They break away from the speakers—first TWO, then ONE—and dance in exhilaration.

TRUBY has straightened up at the sound of the ocean. He sees the dolphins dancing, takes out his recorder and speaks silently into it, making surprised gestures with his free hand.

RUMMEL reprograms the console, presses a switch, and—

Natural dolphin sounds join the ocean sounds: the

sounds of ONE and TWO in the tanks. They can hear each other.

They race back to the speakers, again hanging perfectly still but vibrating.

Breaking away, each dances more excitedly still. TWO races to his side of the platform, leaping up to try to look over the divide between the tanks.

RUMMEL walks over to TRUBY and sits by him, physically closer than the two have ever been, saying nothing for a time, then speaking silently to him.

The two stand and walk down to the tanks, by the platform.

TRUBY begins to throw fish to ONE, bringing her closer and closer to the platform—a replay of GRISSOM with TWO in Act One.

RUMMEL: *[to WATCHERS]* And I had him.

The platform is now to be used as a stretcher, movable by boom and winch. RUMMEL and TRUBY attach ropes to it, and when ONE is right next to it, they slide her onto it and swing it around on the ropes so that ONE is now over TWO's tank.

Suddenly the stretcher/platform shakes and tilts.

TRUBY: The boom snapped!

RUMMEL: Shit in the shallow end!

He and TRUBY wrestle with it, cursing under their breath.

ONE slides off—quite safely—into TWO's tank.

Natural dolphin sounds erupt. The two dolphins are whistling and sonaring back and forth—torrents of sound.

Keeping one eye on the dolphins, RUMMEL examines the broken equipment, then hauls the stretcher/platform up on its ropes, out of the way.

From now on the stage is a single open space.

ONE and TWO start out cautious of each other, skittish, far apart, then gradually begin making little darting movements, closer.

The natural dolphin sounds change to electronic music.

Tentative touching turns into a courtship dance.

TRUBY and RUMMEL have left the tanks to go and sit with the WATCHERS, everyone together for the first time.

They all watch, absorbed in the dolphins' dance of life.

And the courtship dance turns into mating—a long gliding pas de deux, twined bodies rolling and turning.

RUMMEL: *[to WATCHERS]* And I had him. I was certain.

8. THE RETURN OF GRISSOM

Night turns to day.

The electronic music stops abruptly.

ONE and TWO disengage, swimming separately but synchronized.

RUMMEL and TRUBY see GRISSOM coming down the ladder. They stand.

Just before GRISSOM starts to speak, TRUBY ducks out of sight behind WATCHERS, leaving RUMMEL standing by himself.

GRISSOM: Rummel! Rummel! *YOU PUT THE ANIMALS IN TOGETHER!* What *are* you? Great God almighty— we've got you runnin' sessions—that doesn't take a blind bit more brains than the average chimpanzee—*[making hand signals]* Tank-cleanin'—a hamster with a toilet brush—And security—holy hell, minimum wage we can get a veteran, a qualified marksman, happy to have the work—But you—you're runnin' riot—What *are* you? Some kind of—crazed mutant creature of the night?— *YOU PUT THE ANIMALS IN TOGETHER!—*

RUMMEL starts down toward the tanks. GRISSOM holds up his hand.

GRISSOM: *[continuing]* Hold it. Hold it right there. I don't want you near them. No more. That's it for you. Out. Out of the lab. End of the month. Out of my life.

A tumult of electronic tones and natural dolphin sounds, segueing into—

9. EMOTION RECOLLECTED IN CAPTIVITY

Day.

WATCHERS regroup as THE MEDIA, interviewing RUMMEL.

RUMMEL: So of course it was going to look like some half-ass revenge trip, another one of those disgruntled ex-employee things. 'Grissom fired him, and that's why—'

—Do you hold a grudge?

RUMMEL: Against Grissom? Nah, he is what he is, he's genetically hard-wired to be a Grissom.

—I meant Truby.

> *TRUBY stands, giving a press conference for THE MEDIA.*

TRUBY:—A deep personal loss. Truly, I have no words for my grief . . . A death in the family. Worse than that— to have to live with the knowledge that they were abducted, kidnapped—to see the tanks that were their home, where they were happy . . . empty . . . and to know they have been callously delivered up to the sharks.

RUMMEL: *[to the MEDIA]* He came to see me, would you believe. I'd been in about three months. The last person I expected to see.

—What was that like?

RUMMEL: *[continuing, laughs]* He didn't have his tape recorder. It set off the metal detector. All he wanted to talk about was the feasibility study.

—For controlled release?

TRUBY: Yes. Dr. Bamberger's project.

—Were you surprised Bamberger took that kind of contract?

—To develop a controlled release program?

RUMMEL: Not really.

—Bamberger, of all people?

—Mr. Captive Studies?

—Doctor Isolation Tank?

—Him, setting up a controlled release program?

RUMMEL: You don't have to be a dolphin to know which way the tide is running. Bob Dylan. Bamberger has this uncanny ability to echo-locate on grant money. Truby said it, the first day he showed up at the lab—How exactly did he phrase it?—Bamberger—*the* authority on the workings of the profession, the involved system of reciprocal favors, feedback loops within feedback loops—

TRUBY: A construct as handsome and intricate as the whorls of the chambered nautilus.

RUMMEL: Thomas McGuane, actually, talking about corruption in politics. Very perceptive. Captured it perfectly, in my opinion.

TRUBY: A beautifully designed protocol. Sweepingly conceived. Judiciously timed. Two years for development of technology. Five years of pilot studies. Full implementation thereafter, two to six years.

RUMMEL: And Truby gainfully employed for the duration. It's never going to get beyond the pilot studies, you know. In the end they're going to decide against controlled release anyway. All those dollars, and results guaranteed to suit them. A lock. A win, as we say, win situation for Bamberger. And Truby.

—Were you surprised Bamberger hired Truby?

TRUBY: I'm responsible for extinguishing behavioral responses to acoustic and visual stimuli, reducing dependency on human feeding, conditioning to avoid human contact—

RUMMEL: I've had a lot of time to think about Truby. I mean, I don't think about him all the time—twenty minutes max, first Tuesday of the month. That's plenty for him. I came to the conclusion that Truby is a lab animal himself. Wonderfully well adapted to the work. He's a shallow water creature, he thrives in the pollution. What you call an opportunistic feeder—he'll swallow anything you feed him and never puke it back up. He will take abuse. Throw dead fish at him and he'll come back for more . . . For the Bamberger protocol of life, he fits the technical specs to perfection . . . Yeah, he's a real lab specimen. *Laboratorius opportunisticus trubius* . . .   But then I thought, one Tuesday afternoon—nah, that's an insult to dolphins.

He turns to TRUBY, and THE MEDIA do too.

RUMMEL: *[continuing, in TRUBY's face]* Truby's a remora. He's a little sucker fish that travels with one big shark, gets to hang out with the heavies, go all kinds of places in the world it would never make it to by itself, all the way to the top of the food chain. Fastens onto the big shark with its suckers, and the only move it ever makes on it own, it swims in and out of the shark's jaws and eats out the bits stuck between its teeth.

During this, TRUBY has turned away, clicking his recorder on and off. Now he swings and faces RUMMEL.

TRUBY: What makes you the chosen one, Rummel? Who says you get to make the decision for the whole world? All the scientists who have spent their whole careers studying marine mammals, and the ones who approve Dr. Bamberger's grants—they're the *authorities*—what gives you the right to decide for all the dolphins in the ocean and all the people and all life on earth that I and Dr. Bamberger shouldn't be able to go on with our work?

RUMMEL: *[to THE MEDIA]* There you have it—the Full Truby. He can open that remora mouth of his, and flap those sucker-fish lips, and fasten onto the soft option and the high moral ground in one suck. And get rewarded for it.

He stands and looks down at TRUBY.

RUMMEL: *[continuing]* Does he really think I couldn't figure it out? That he told Bamberger it was me that did it? Truby's First Law of Limited Involvement: 'Don't Get Any On You.' Does he really think I don't know that's how he got the job? Well, right on, Truby. His behavior got positive-reinforced. Give him a fish.

He throws a fish at TRUBY like a quarterback rifling a pass. TRUBY flinches, but not much.

RUMMEL: *[continuing]* He'll get on, he'll rise in the world. Cream and bastards rise. Frederic Raphael. But he'll always be Truby, and that's a life sentence. That will be his punishment.

He turns away from TRUBY to the MEDIA.

RUMMEL: *[continuing]* I never saw him again . . . Never saw the dolphins again either . . . I think about them all the time . . .

—You saw the papers, though.

—The six o'clock news.

—Dolphins harassing the fishermen.

—That was my story.

—Hey, that was *my* story.

—Two of them.

—They hide outside the night light.

—One of them pulls on the anchor line and rocks the boat—

RUMMEL: That sounds like Two.

—And if the fishermen beat them to the catch they snap the line.

RUMMEL: It never was a good idea to get between One and the fish bucket.

   Pause.

—So you don't think they're dead?

RUMMEL: There's a chance they are. Of course there is. But I wanted them to have a chance to live like dolphins. Not in the tank. In the ocean.

—And how are you handling it yourself?

RUMMEL: Life in the tank? Sometimes—say, first Thursday of the month—I think it might be more fun in those big old dolphin holding pens. At least I'd be hearing a better grade of war story. Here it's mostly dudes that hit the 711 with an Uzi and they don't even have the smarts to score some Twinkies so they can plead the sugar rush defense. But think what you've got in the holding pens. Veterans of foreign wars. Scars on their beaks. The dolphins that recovered the A-bomb that fell out of the B-52. The ones that were supposed to off Castro out scuba diving. The really old ones, Vietnam vets—the Swimmer Nullification program—now *there* was an operant conditioning protocol. Sonar the enemy frogman, jab him in the ass with the CO_2 cartridge and the industrial-strength syringe on the beak—and you have one truly surprised inflating frogman—blows up like a balloon, the body bobs up to the surface to be body-counted . . .

—Here, though?

—Day by day?

RUMMEL: Boring, boring. boring. Mainly only sensory invariety. Enough room to move around, though. No stereotyped behavior. So far. And I've learned to whistle out the side of my mouth.

—Have you had any offers?

—For your story?

RUMMEL: Sure. But—Movie of the Week? Nah. 'Fools'

names and fools' faces are often seen in public places.'
Benjamin Franklin. Anyway, it's been done. The story's
been told.

—What do you mean?

RUMMEL: Dig. You have this alien creature. Strange.
Intelligent. Interesting. Means no harm to humans. These
high-tech scientists want to capture it and study it. It
wants to go home. Some good little low-tech kids help it
escape.

Pause.

RUMMEL: *[continuing]* I play the tones. I delay. I play the
question tone. Is this tone the same?

Pause.

—ET?

—*[overlapping]* ET!

RUMMEL: Correct. Give them a fish. Great movie, something the whole family can enjoy, teaches kids the right
lessons. And it makes half a billion dollars. Meanwhile,
back in the real world, me in my low-budget home movie,
I get my ass in a sling . . . Well, as the raven said, Never
mind. I took the dolphins, I get to take the consequences.

—You still have quite a while to go—

—Are you working toward—

—Early release—

—For good behavior?

RUMMEL: It's a question, isn't it? Am I a One or a Two? I think about it, twenty minutes every Sunday. I don't know . . . But I'll tell you one thing. If I was here for life, and they opened the gate and told me, 'OK, it's a dangerous world out there, a jungle. So, your choice—you can stay here and be safe, till you die, or you can run for the woods, and if you make it you're free, only in thirty seconds we start shooting' . . . I'd go for it.

THE LAW: Five minutes. Last questions.

—Why did you do it?

—Why did you take the dolphins out of the tanks?

Pause.

RUMMEL: Because they were there.

Pause.

—*How* did you do it?

—You never testified—

—If the boom was broken, how—

—Truby's deposition says you were calm—

RUMMEL: Calm? Every time I noticed my hands they were running through my hair.

—Did you have it all worked out ahead of time?

RUMMEL: Sure. In my head. I had the Navy manual on transporting dolphins, bedside reading, and I had it memorized. To the syllable. I read it every week. For a year. But on the night—hell, I was just trying to keep enough shirt on to finish the shift.

10. OUT OF THE TANK

Night.

RUMMEL goes to the imaginary telephone that he used in Act One to phone his friends to come to the party. He makes silent calls. TRUBY watches as —

THE MEDIA regroup as FRIENDS OF RUMMEL.

—Hey.

—Wanna come down to the beach?

—Sure. Who's going to be there?

—Just us.

—And the dolphins.

—Are you up for tonight?

—Why—what's happening?

—Want to go for a swim? With a couple of dolphins?

—In the ocean.

—In the ocean?

—There's some heavy lifting.

—They ain't heavy, they're dolphins.

—So I said to him, I'm busy.

—And—

—And he said, Whatever it is, drop it. So I did.

—Are you in?

—I'm in.

—I'm in.

ONE and TWO have been quiescent on the trapezes in the center of the tanks.

RUMMEL opens the drain valves to start the water level going down.

RUMMEL: *[to the DOLPHINS]* One more time. For the good times.

FRIENDS are assembling.

RUMMEL: *[mostly to himself]* Check the tide tables. Tide turns at midnight. That makes—water down by 10.30 at the latest. So, start draining at 6.30. Padding, foam, for the truck. Water. Sponges to keep them wetted down.

FRIENDS have assembled. RUMMEL speaks directly to them now.

RUMMEL: OK. We only get one shot at this, so it has to go by the clock. Fifteen minutes each dolphin, tank to transport. An hour on the road. Midnight, down to the water.

—And security comes around every hour on the hour, right?

RUMMEL: By the gates, yeah. I've timed it—they'll be over the far side when we move out. Oh yeah, one other thing. There's a guy, lives in the dumpster by the cannery. If he pops his head out when you go past and says, 'Watch out for Saddam,' don't panic, it's just stereotyped behavior, he'll be fine, you'll be fine.

—You'll be fine.

—Hold on.

—Not long now.

—Easy.

—The last time.

—Steady, steady.

From here, the dolphins are being moved out of the tanks, supported by RUMMEL and FRIENDS. TWO goes first, and when it is ONE's turn, TWO becomes a human helper.

While this is going on, THE LAW interposes, and everybody freezes.

THE LAW: The defendant argues what he grandiosely refers to as the rights of the dolphins. But in law, animals in the wild have no rights. They are outside the law, outlaws. Once in captivity, all rights are with the owner—property rights. These are the only rights that can be injured.

In motion again.

—OK, black line.

—Watch the pecs.

—Keep her wet.

—Get the truck started.

Freeze as THE LAW speaks again.

THE LAW: What the defendant takes it upon himself to call liberation, the court defines as theft. The dolphins were property, the property of the owner. The defendant, without authorization, deprived the owner of his property. That is an element of theft.

11. DOWN THE BEACH AND INTO THE SEA

Straight on, in motion again.

—Listen.

—They can tell they're almost there.

—They can hear the surf—

—On the reef.

—Fifty yards.

—Tide's up.

—Lights. Over there. What—?

—Watch it. Steady.

—Slippery.

—Seaweed.

—What's that? Over there?

—Under the trees?

—Just fishermen.

—No, no, down the other side.

—What are those lights?

—There. In the trees.

—What's that noise?

—It's kids, kids in a van.

—Making out.

—Disgusting.

—You're being anthropomorphic.

—Keep going.

—Watch out for that pec.

—We're at the shallows.

—OK, let them go.

—Let them go.

—No—

—Don't let them go till they can swim free . . .

THE LAW: The final element is intent. Was the intent to deprive?

RUMMEL, among FRIENDS, holding a dolphin, raises his head and looks directly at THE LAW.

RUMMEL: To deprive? What do you call what was done to the dolphins? What was their crime? Being a dolphin? What was the punishment? Captivity, isolation for life? What's the word for that? Would you call that depriving?

THE LAW: Confine yourself to the question. As to the laboratory—Was the intent to deprive?

Pause.

RUMMEL: Yes.

12. AND THEY JUST SWAM AWAY

Straight on.

RUMMEL and FRIENDS retreat from the tank space—now the open sea—and watch as the DOLPHINS dance.

Speech fragments, quieter and with more time between utterances as they go along.

—I'm going in with them.

—No.

—Let them go.

—Hey, over there.

—I can't see them.

—There's a gap in the reef.

—The channel.

—They'll find it.

—I can hear one of them—

—Breathing.

—Look. They're surfing.

—Is that them? Over there?

—Where?

—I see a fin.

—I think . . .

—Over there.

—Way out . . .

—Maybe they won't go. Maybe they'll come back.

—No.

—Would you?

—They're gone.

—I can't believe—

—They're gone.

—They're gone.

—They just swam away . . .

*Open ocean sounds and natural dolphin sounds come
up and continue as RUMMEL speaks.*

RUMMEL: The first time I ever saw a dolphin was in
high school. We were out at the point, Pray For Sex
Beach, and we saw a fin. We thought it must be a shark.
It was only shallow, so we waded in and threw stones.
But it wasn't a shark, it was a dolphin. It was whistling.
It came up to me and leaned against my leg. And I
thought, What's with this dolphin, is it sick or something? It kept following us. It was only a small one, so we
picked it up and carried it into a little lagoon. I called
Marineland, and they said when a dolphin comes ashore
there's nothing you can do, they die . . . We stayed with

it, sprinkled water on it to keep it wet. It just whistled and whistled. It got dark. And the dolphin died . . . We came back at the weekend, and the body was all puffed up from the sun, and people were throwing rocks at it, kids were poking it in the eye with sticks . . . It was strange. It could have gone anywhere, any beach up and down the coast. But—we were the only ones on the beach, and it came to where we were. It wasn't looking for a beach. It was looking for company, it was looking for comfort . . . Now, I don't want you to think that was my Road to Damascus or anything like that . . . But it's something I remember . . .

The sound level rises.

ALL are watching absorbed as the DOLPHINS dance in the open ocean.

Lights fade to black, sound continues, then fades, dolphins in the distance, then gone altogether . . . silence . . . and . . .

CURTAIN

ACKNOWLEDGEMENTS

My grateful thanks to Tom Farber of El León, for paying me the compliment of choosing my work to be part of his new imprint. Tom spends as much time as possible in the water, and so does *Bite The Hand*—for me, a happy affinity.

A first version of this piece was workshopped and staged in Australia, under the title *Dolphin Play*, at the Mill Theatre, Geelong, transferring to the Australian Contemporary Theatre, Melbourne. From that production just one element remains, the dolphin movement. Since then the text has gone through many evolutionary changes, to the point where it has become a distinct new species, properly with its own name, *Bite The Hand*.

Going back to the origin, I thank the people of the Mill. Artistic director James McCaughey, for taking a deep breath and risking something distinctly not run of the mill. Choreographer Nan Hassall, who by successive approximations shaped actors untrained in movement into dancers, and then transformed dancers into dolphins. Les Gilbert, who assembled electronic soundscapes out of dolphin clicks and whistles. Neil Greenaway, who designed costumes adaptable to terrestrial mammals who turn into marine mammals and back again. And special thanks to aerialist Rinski Ginsberg of Circus Oz (a precursor to Cirque Du Soleil in revolutionizing circus entertainment), for her inspired re-imagining of the trapeze, its philosophy and practice.

The two dolphins who danced so beautifully and powerfully in the tanks were Bernadette Fitzgerald and Daryl Pellizer. The others who changed species on command were Angela Chaplin, Tom Considine, Elena Eremin, Matthew Fargher, William Henderson, and Lisa Scott-Murphy, each of them distinct and engaging in stage personality and dolphinality. To all, my thanks.

And thanks, from the beginning and always, to my wife, Carolyn Yukiko. She knows why.